CATCH-UP MATH

Get your child back on track!

- Skip Counting • Place Value • Addition
- Subtraction • Regrouping • Graphs
- Shapes • Fractions • Length
- Time • Money

Author
Christine Dugan, M.A.Ed.

Consultant
Angela Gallo, M.A.Ed.
Richardson Independent School District

Publishing Credits
Corinne Burton, M.A.Ed., *President and Publisher*
Gabe Thibodeau, *Content Director*
Véronique Bos, *VP of Creative*
Lynette Ordoñez, *Content Manager*
Melissa Laughlin, *Editor*
Kevin Pham, *Graphic Designer*

Image Credits all images from iStock and/or Shutterstock

Standards
© Copyright 2010 National Governors Association Center for Best Practices and Council of Chief State School Officers. All rights reserved.
© Copyright 2007–2022 Texas Education Agency (TEA). All Rights Reserved.
© 2024 TESOL International Association
© 2024 Board of Regents of the University of Wisconsin System

The classroom teacher may reproduce copies of materials in this book for classroom use only. The reproduction of any part for an entire school or school system is strictly prohibited. No part of this publication may be transmitted, stored, or recorded in any form without written permission from the publisher.

Website addresses included in this book are public domain and may be subject to changes or alterations of content after publication of this product. Shell Education does not take responsibility for the future accuracy or relevance and appropriateness of website addresses included in this book. Please contact the company if you come across any inappropriate or inaccurate website addresses, and they will be corrected in product reprints.

All companies, websites, and products mentioned in this book are registered trademarks of their respective owners or developers and are used in this book strictly for editorial purposes. No commercial claim to their use is made by the author(s) or the publisher.

A division of Teacher Created Materials

5482 Argosy Avenue
Huntington Beach, CA 92649
www.tcmpub.com/shell-education
ISBN 979-8-7659-8215-0
© 2025 Shell Educational Publishing, Inc.
Printed by: 51497
Printed in: China

Contents

About Catch-Up Math................5
How to Use the QR Codes in
Catch-Up Math....................6
Math Skills........................7

1. WHOLE NUMBERS

Read and Write Whole Numbers.......9
Count by Tens.....................11
Count by Fives...................13
Count by Twenty-Fives............15
Count by Hundreds................17
Odd and Even Numbers.............19
Add Odd and Even Numbers........21
One-Step Word Problems..........23
Two-Step Word Problems..........26
Expanded Form...................30
Order Numbers...................33
Whole Numbers Review............35

2. MENTAL MATH

Fact Families to 20..............38
Count On........................40
Count Back......................43
Make Tens.......................45
Doubles + or – 1................48
Commutative Property............50
Addition Facts to 20............52
Subtraction Facts to 20.........55
Mental Math Review..............57

3. PLACE VALUE

Tens and Ones...................61
Greater Than, Less Than, Equal To...64
Compare Three-Digit Numbers.....67
10 More and 10 Less.............70
100 More and 100 Less...........73
Place Value Review..............76

4. ADDITION

Add One- and Two-Digit Numbers....79
Use Base-Ten Blocks..............82
Addition with Number Lines......85
Add Tens and Ones...............88
Unknown Addends.................90
Add Three Numbers...............92
Addition with Regrouping........95
Standard Addition Algorithm.....98
Add Three-Digit Numbers........101
Addition Review................104

5. SUBTRACTION

Subtract One-Digit Numbers from
Two-Digit Numbers..............110
Subtraction with Base-Ten Blocks....113
Subtraction with Number Lines..116
Subtract Tens and Ones.........119
Add to Subtract................121
Subtraction with Regrouping....123
Standard Subtraction Algorithm....126
Subtraction with Three-Digit
Numbers.......................129
Subtraction Review.............132

Contents

6. DATA AND GRAPHS

Charts....................137
Picture Graphs...............141
Bar Graphs..................145
Line Plots..................150
Data and Graphs Review..........155

7. SHAPES AND ARRAYS

Shape Attributes..............159
Make New Shapes..............161
Understanding Arrays...........164
Arrays with Rectangles..........166
Add Arrays..................168
Shapes and Arrays Review........170

8. FRACTIONS

Equal Parts.................172
Partition Rectangles............174
Partition Circles..............176
Naming Fractions..............178
Fractions Review..............181

9. LENGTH

Measurement Tools.............184
Measurement Units.............187
Inches and Centimeters..........190
Compare Lengths..............192
Estimate Lengths..............195
Length Word Problems..........197
Length Review................199

10. TIME AND MONEY

Digital Clocks................205
Analog Clocks: 00 and 30........207
Analog Clocks: 15 and 45........209
Five-Minute Intervals...........211
Elapsed Time.................213
Adding Coins.................215
Money Word Problems..........217
Time and Money Review.........219

ANSWERS

1 Whole Numbers Answers......223
2 Mental Math Answers.........226
3 Place Value Answers..........229
4 Addition Answers............232
5 Subtraction Answers..........235
6 Data and Graphs Answers......238
7 Shapes and Arrays Answers....241
8 Fractions Answers............243
9 Length Answers..............244
10 Time and Money Answers.....246

About Catch-Up Math

The **Catch-Up Math** series enables children to start from scratch when they are struggling with grade-level math. Each book takes math back to the foundation and ensures that all basic concepts are consolidated before moving forward. Lots of revision and opportunities to practice and build confidence are provided before moving on to new topics.

Each new topic is introduced clearly with simple explanations, examples, and trial questions (with answers) before children move to the Practice section. To help students understand difficult topics, instructional videos are included throughout the book.

This book has 10 chapters that cover a variety of mathematical concepts. The chapters are:

1. Whole Numbers
2. Mental Math
3. Place Value
4. Addition
5. Subtraction
6. Data and Graphs
7. Shapes and Arrays
8. Fractions
9. Length
10. Time and Money

A QR code on a topic page provides access to the video.

Each Your Turn section contains a SELF CHECK for students to use for reflection and self-assessment.

★ A review section that can be used as an assessment and to check children's progress is included at the end of each chapter.

★ Answers are at the back of the book.

How to Use This Book

Children can work through the pages from front to back or choose individual topics to reinforce areas where they are struggling.

The topics are introduced with:

- clear instructions, using simple language

- completed examples and incomplete examples for students to tackle before moving on to the **Your Turn** sections

- videos linked by QR codes to provide additional instruction and clarify difficult concepts

© Shell Education 146444—Catch-Up Math 5

How to Use the QR Codes in Catch-Up Math

A unique aspect of the **Catch-Up Math** series is the instructional videos.

The videos further explain and clarify various mathematical concepts. The videos are simply accessed via QR codes and can be watched on a phone or tablet. Or, view all the videos by following this link: tcmpub.digital/cumath2.

Access the video by scanning the QR code with your device.

Each video shows the page from the book. An instructor talks through the concepts and examples and demonstrates what children need to do. The solutions to the examples are presented before children tackle the **Your Turn** sections. This careful instruction ensures that children can confidently move on to the following Practice questions. Children should be encouraged to check their **Your Turn** answers before moving on.

10 instructional videos included!

After watching the video, children can confidently complete the **Your Turn** section.

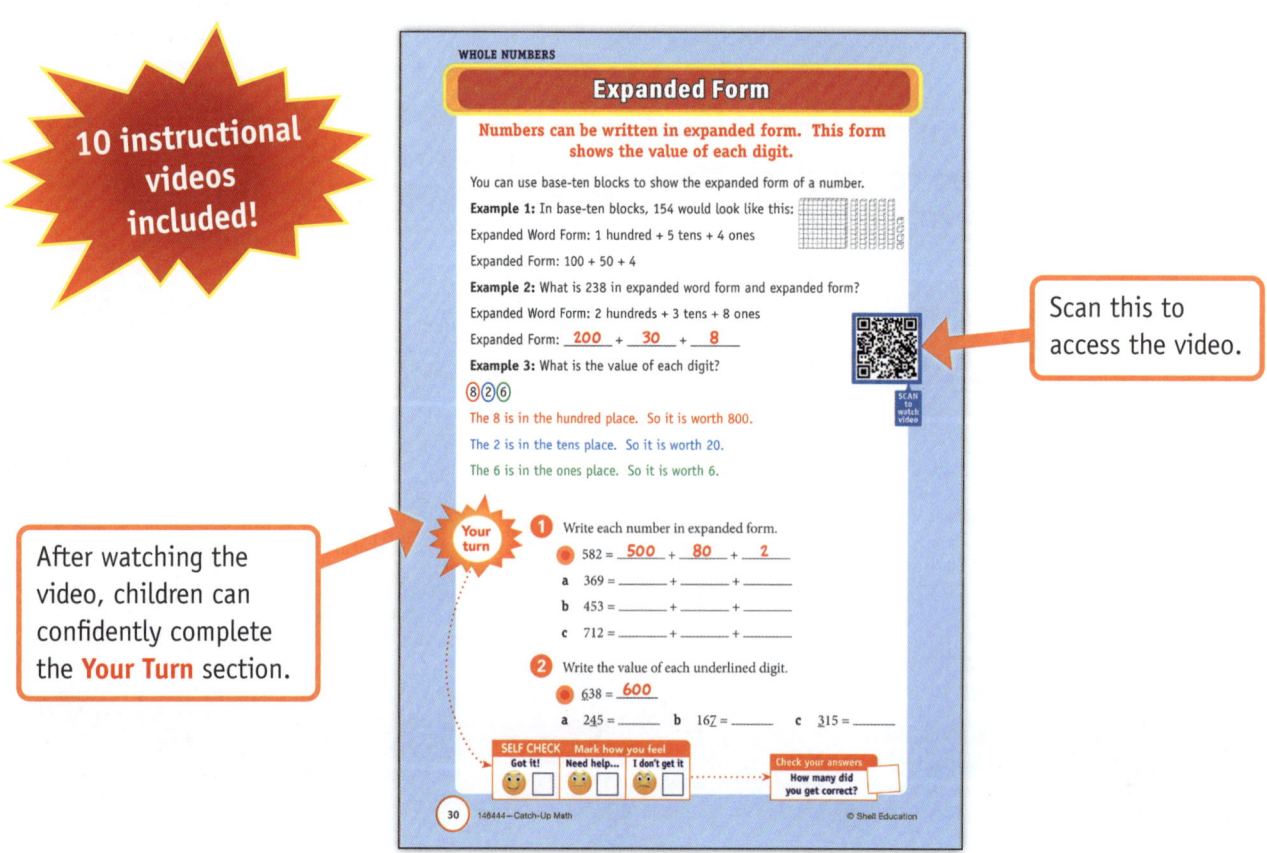

Scan this to access the video.

Math Skills

This book contains key math skills from both first and second grade to help your child recap and catch up to grade level.

Grade 1 Math Skills	Pages
Count to 120, starting at any number. Represent a number of objects with a written numeral.	9–22
Add and subtract within 20 to solve word problems.	23–29
Compare two two-digit numbers, using the symbols >, =, and <.	33–34, 64–69
Relate counting to addition and subtraction.	40–44
Use properties of operations to add and subtract.	50–51
Add and subtract within 20, and fluently add and subtract within 10.	38–56, 110–122
Understand that the two digits of a two-digit number represent amounts of tens and ones.	61–75
Mentally find 10 more or 10 less than a two-digit number.	70–72
Add within 100, including adding a two-digit number and a one-digit number, and adding a two-digit number and a multiple of 10.	79–103
Understand subtraction as an unknown-addend problem.	121–122
Solve word problems that call for addition of three whole numbers.	92–94
Use fact families to add and subtract.	38–39
Organize, represent, and interpret data with up to three categories. Ask and answer questions about the data.	137–154
Build and draw shapes to have certain attributes.	159–163
Compose shapes to create a composite shape.	161–163
Partition circles and rectangles into two and four equal shares.	172–177
Compare and order three objects by length.	192–194
Tell and write time in hours and half-hours, using analog and digital clocks.	205–208
Identify the values of pennies, nickels, dimes, and quarters.	215–216

Math Skills

Grade 2 Math Skills	Pages
Read and write numbers to 1,000 using numerals, words, and expanded form.	9–10, 30–34
Skip-count by 5s, 10s, 25s, and 100s.	11–18
Determine whether a group has an odd or even number of objects.	21–22
Add and subtract within 100 to solve one- and two-step word problems.	23–29
Compare three-digit numbers.	67–69
Fluently add and subtract within 20 using mental strategies.	38–56
Understand that the digits of a three-digit number represent amounts of hundreds, tens, and ones.	61–75
Mentally add or subtract 10 or 100 to a given number less than 1,000.	70–75
Fluently add and subtract within 100.	79–100, 110–128
Use strategies to add and subtract within 1,000.	101–103, 129–131
Draw a picture graph or bar graph to represent data. Solve problems using a bar graph.	141–149
Use a line plot to represent data.	150–154
Recognize and draw shapes that have certain attributes.	159–163
Add to find the total number of objects in an array.	164–169
Partition a rectangle into rows and columns of same-size squares. Count to find the total number of them.	166–167
Partition circles and rectangles into 2, 3, or 4 equal shares.	172–180
Use appropriate tools to measure length.	184–186
Use a ruler to measure length to the nearest inch or centimeter.	190–191
Measure to find how much longer one object is than another.	192–194
Estimate lengths using units of inches, feet, centimeters, and meters.	195–196
Solve word problems involving lengths.	197–198
Use analog and digital clocks to tell and write time to the nearest five minutes.	205–212
Solve problems involving elapsed time.	213–214
Solve word problems involving dollar bills, quarters, dimes, nickels, and pennies.	215–218

WHOLE NUMBERS

Read and Write Whole Numbers

Whole numbers are the numbers that you count. A whole number is made up of digits.

Numbers are often shown as digits, such as 1, 2, and 3. Numbers can also be shown as words. The number 22 can be written as *twenty-two*.

Example 1: Write 156 in words.   **one hundred fifty-six**

Example 2: Write seventy-two as a number.   **72**

Use these terms to write numbers in word form.

Tens	Ones
ten	one
twenty	two
thirty	three
forty	four
fifty	five
sixty	six
seventy	seven
eighty	eight
ninety	nine

Use a hyphen to write 21 to 99 in words. For example, 45 is written as forty-five.

Your turn

1. Write the numbers or words.

● 154 __one hundred fifty-four__

a 46 _____

b _____ two hundred twenty

c 88 _____

d _____ seventy-three

SELF CHECK Mark how you feel

Got it!   Need help...   I don't get it

Check your answers

How many did you get correct?

WHOLE NUMBERS

Practice

1 Write the words as numbers.

● twenty-five __25__

a ninety-two _____

b sixty-five _____

c twenty-three _____

d twelve _____

e ninety-nine _____

f fifty-nine _____

g one hundred thirty-four _____

h two hundred seventy-two _____

i three hundred forty _____

j one hundred seven _____

k five hundred eleven _____

2 Write the numbers as words.

● 43 __forty-three__

a 31 _____

b 87 _____

c 25 _____

d 55 _____

e 60 _____

f 143 _____

g 215 _____

h 378 _____

i 201 _____

j 450 _____

WHOLE NUMBERS

Count by Tens

When you count by tens, you count every 10th number.

Example 1: Start at 0, and count by tens. All the numbers will end in 0.

10, 20, 30, 40…

Example 2: You can also count by tens when you start at any number. This means you add 10 more.

1, 11, 21, 31…

Example 3: You can also count backward by tens.

90, 80, 70, 60…

1	2	3	4	5	6	7	8	9	10
11	12	13	14	15	16	17	18	19	20
21	22	23	24	25	26	27	28	29	30
31	32	33	34	35	36	37	38	39	40
41	42	43	44	45	46	47	48	49	50
51	52	53	54	55	56	57	58	59	60
61	62	63	64	65	66	67	68	69	70
71	72	73	74	75	76	77	78	79	80
81	82	83	84	85	86	87	88	89	90
91	92	93	94	95	96	97	98	99	100

Look for patterns when counting by tens. The number in the tens place changes. The number in the ones place does not.

Your turn

1 Count by tens. Write the missing numbers.

● 20, 30, __40__, __50__, 60

a 30, 40, _____, 60, _____

b _____, 21, 31, 41, _____

SELF CHECK Mark how you feel

Got it!   Need help…   I don't get it

Check your answers — How many did you get correct?

WHOLE NUMBERS

Practice

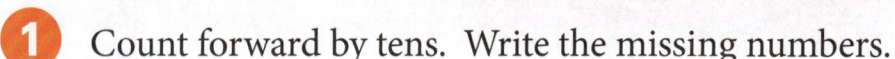

1 Count forward by tens. Write the missing numbers.

● 10, **20**, **30**, 40, **50**, 60

a 30, ____, 50, ____, 70, 80

b 10, ____, ____, 40, ____, ____

c 20, ____, ____, ____, 60, 70

d 50, ____, ____, ____, 90, 100

e 40, ____, ____, ____, ____, 90

2 Count backward by tens. Write the missing numbers.

● 80, 70, 60, **50**, **40**, **30**

a 70, ____, ____, 40, 30, ____

b 90, 80, ____, ____, 50, 40

c 40, ____, ____, ____, 0

d 80, ____, 60, ____, 40, ____

e 60, ____, ____, ____, ____, 10

3 Count by tens to complete each column in the hundred chart.

1	2	3	4		6	7	8	9	10
11	12	13	14		16	17			20
21		23	24		26	27	28		30
31		33	34			37			
41		43	44	45		47	48		
51		53	54	55		57			
61			64	65	66	67	68	69	
71			74	75	76			79	
81			84	85	86		88	89	
91		93	94	95	96			99	

WHOLE NUMBERS

Count by Fives

You can count by fives. This means you count every 5th number, or add 5 each time.

Example 1: Count forward by fives.

5, 10, 15, 20, 25…
 +5 +5 +5 +5

Example 2: Count backward by fives.

50, 45, 40, 35, 30…
 −5 −5 −5 −5

> When you count by 5s, the numbers always end with a 5 or a 0.

Your turn

1 Count forward or backward by fives. Write the missing numbers.

● 30, 35, 40, __45__, __50__, 55

a 0, 5, _____, _____, 20, 25

b 45, 50, 55, _____, 65, _____

c 95, 90, 85, _____, _____, _____

d 65, _____, 55, _____, _____, 40

SELF CHECK Mark how you feel

Got it!  Need help…  I don't get it

Check your answers
How many did you get correct?

WHOLE NUMBERS

Practice

1 Count forward or backward by fives. Write the missing numbers.

● 30, __35__, 40, __45__, 50, __55__

a 5, 10, _____, _____, 25, 30

b 25, _____, 35, _____, 45, _____

c 65, _____, 55, _____, 45, _____

d 15, _____, _____, _____, _____, 40

e 10, _____, _____, _____, _____, 35

f 50, _____, _____, _____, _____, 75

g 90, _____, _____, _____, _____, 65

h 40, _____, _____, _____, _____, 15

2 Count by fives. Color each number you count in red.

1	2	3	4	5	6	7	8	9	10
11	12	13	14	15	16	17	18	19	20
21	22	23	24	25	26	27	28	29	30
31	32	33	34	35	36	37	38	39	40
41	42	43	44	45	46	47	48	49	50
51	52	53	54	55	56	57	58	59	60
61	62	63	64	65	66	67	68	69	70
71	72	73	74	75	76	77	78	79	80
81	82	83	84	85	86	87	88	89	90
91	92	93	94	95	96	97	98	99	100

WHOLE NUMBERS

Count by Twenty-Fives

You can count by 25s. You count every 25th number, or add 25 each time.

Example 1: You can use a number line. Start at 0. Then, count by 25s.

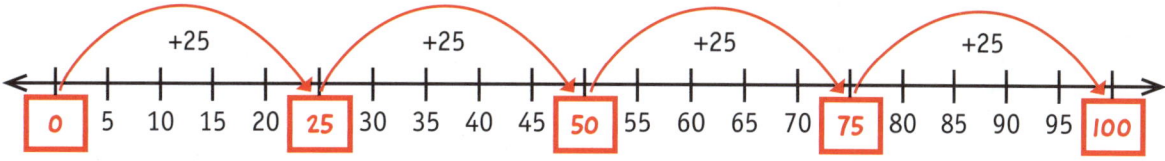

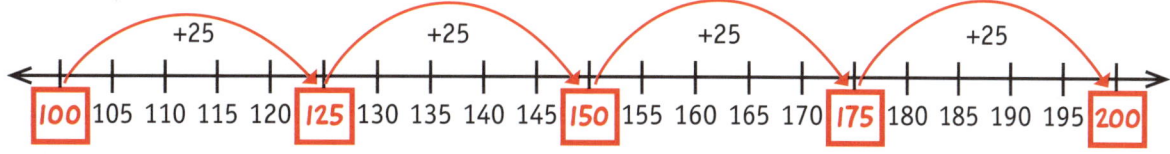

Example 2: Once you see the pattern, you can skip count by 25s without a number line.

25, 50, 75, 100, 125, 150, 175, 200, 225, 250, **275**, **300**

1 Count by 25s. Write the missing numbers.

● 75, 100, 125, __150__, __175__

a 200, 225, _____, _____, _____

b 450, 475, 500, _____, _____

c 700, 725, 750, _____, _____

d 575, 600, _____, _____, _____

SELF CHECK Mark how you feel
Got it!   Need help...   I don't get it

Check your answers
How many did you get correct?

WHOLE NUMBERS

Practice

1 Count by 25s. Write the missing numbers.

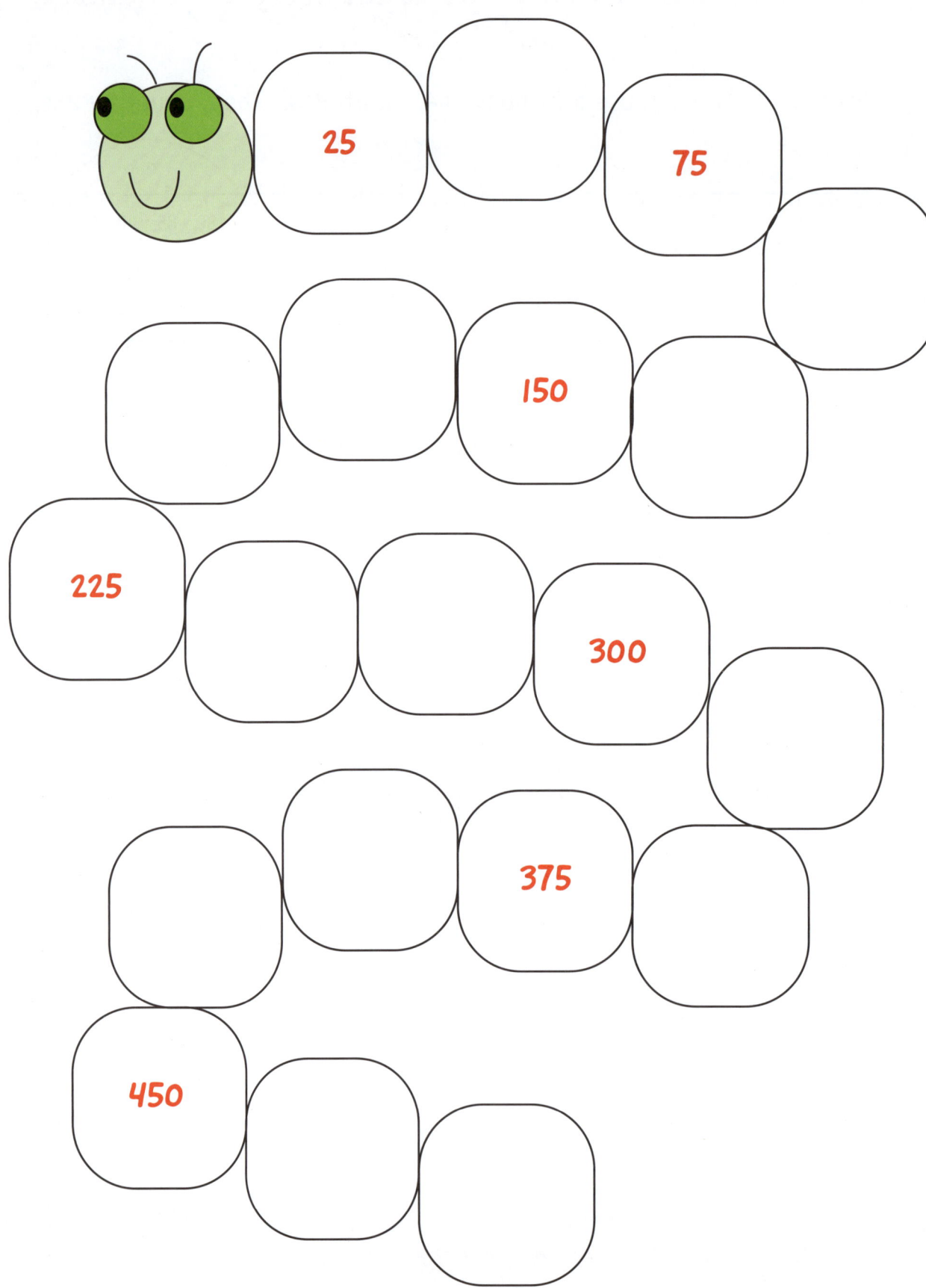

WHOLE NUMBERS

Count by Hundreds

You can count by 100s. You count every 100th number, or you add 100 every time.

Example 1: Count forward by 100s.

100, 200, 300, 400, 500...

Example 2: Count backward by 100s.

600, 500, 400, 300, 200...

Example 3: You can count by 100s starting at any number.

125, 225, 325, **425, 525**

How would you count by 100s if you started at 150?

1 Count by 100s. Write the missing numbers.

● 100, 200, __300__, __400__, 500

a 300, _____, _____, 600, _____

b 100, _____, 300, _____, _____

c 700, 600, _____, _____, _____

d 900, 800, _____, _____, _____

SELF CHECK Mark how you feel

Got it!  □   Need help...  □   I don't get it  □

Check your answers
How many did you get correct?

© Shell Education

WHOLE NUMBERS

Practice

1 Solve the problems. Count forward by 100.

● 500 + 100 = __600__

a 300 + 100 = _____

b 600 + 100 = _____

c 200 + 100 = _____

d 100 + 100 = _____

e 400 + 100 = _____

f 825 + 100 = _____

g 742 + 100 = _____

2 Solve the problems. Count backward by 100.

● 300 − 100 = __200__

a 400 − 100 = _____

b 300 − 100 = _____

c 700 − 100 = _____

d 100 − 100 = _____

e 500 − 100 = _____

f 806 − 100 = _____

g 210 − 100 = _____

3 Count by 100s to write the missing numbers.

● 100, __200__, __300__, __400__, 500, 600

a 800, _____, 600, _____, _____, _____

b 400, _____, _____, _____, 800, _____

c 122, _____, _____, _____, 522, _____

d 500, _____, _____, _____, _____, 1,000

WHOLE NUMBERS

Odd and Even Numbers

An even number can be divided into two equal groups. An odd number cannot be divided into two equal groups.

Example 1: Even numbers end with a 0, 2, 4, 6, or 8. 6 is an even number.

two equal groups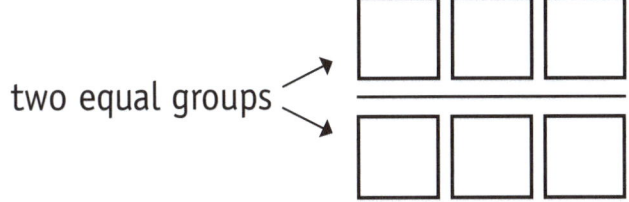

When an odd number is split into 2 groups, there is 1 left over.

Example 2: Odd numbers end with a 1, 3, 5, 7, or 9. 7 is an odd number.

two unequal groups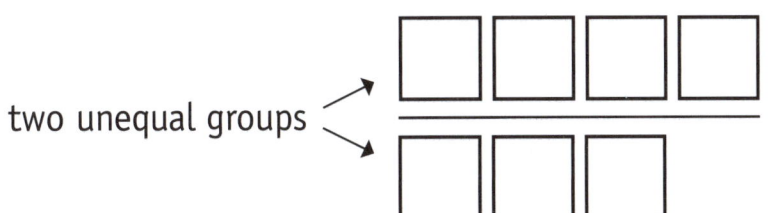

1 Circle whether each number is odd or even.

•	11	(odd) even	c	25	odd even
a	8	odd even	d	57	odd even
b	14	odd even	e	32	odd even

SELF CHECK Mark how you feel

Got it!  Need help...   I don't get it

Check your answers How many did you get correct?

WHOLE NUMBERS

Practice

1 Draw pictures to show each number. Split them into 2 groups. Then, write whether the number is odd or even.

● 4 is _even_ .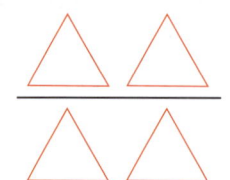

b 12 is _____ .

a 5 is _____ .

c 7 is _____ .

2 Complete each task.

● Write all of the odd numbers between 0 and 10.

_1   3   5   7   9_

a Write all of the even numbers between 20 and 30.

_____

b Write all of the odd numbers between 50 and 60.

_____

c Write all of the even numbers between 44 and 54.

_____

3 Circle the even numbers. Underline the odd numbers.

1	2	3	4	5	6	7	8	9	10
11	12	13	14	15	16	17	18	19	20
21	22	23	24	25	26	27	28	29	30

WHOLE NUMBERS

Add Odd and Even Numbers

You can predict whether a sum will be even or odd.

Example 1: When you add two even numbers, the answer, or sum, is always even.

4 + 8 = 12

Example 2: When you add two odd numbers, the sum is always even.

3 + 7 = 10

Example 3: When you add an odd number and an even number, the sum is always odd.

14 + 5 = 19

Example 4: A *double* is when you add the same number to itself. The sum of a double is always an even number.

Add a double of odd numbers.   5 + 5 = **10**

Add a double of even numbers.   8 + 8 = **16**

Why do you think an odd number plus an odd number is always even?

Your turn

1 Solve the doubles problems.

• 6 + 6 = **12**

a 2 + 2 = _____

b 10 + 10 = _____

c 7 + 7 = _____

d 9 + 9 = _____

e 4 + 4 = _____

f 13 + 13 = _____

SELF CHECK Mark how you feel

Got it!   Need help...   I don't get it

Check your answers
How many did you get correct?

21

WHOLE NUMBERS

Practice

1 Solve the doubles problems.

● 7 + 7 = __14__

a 11 + 11 = _____

b 4 + 4 = _____

c 20 + 20 = _____

d 6 + 6 = _____

e 8 + 8 = _____

f 5 + 5 = _____

g 15 + 15 = _____

2 Circle the problems that have even sums. Underline the problems with odd sums.

3 + 4   2 + 22   19 + 19   78 + 66

7 + 29   26 + 45   11 + 14   31 + 101

3 Write addition equations with even sums.

● __3__ + __3__ = __6__

a _____ + _____ = _____

b _____ + _____ = _____

c _____ + _____ = _____

4 Write addition equations with odd sums.

● __12__ + __3__ = __15__

a _____ + _____ = _____

b _____ + _____ = _____

c _____ + _____ = _____

22   146444—Catch-Up Math   © Shell Education

WHOLE NUMBERS

One-Step Word Problems

A one-step word problem is a problem that you solve in a single step.

Read word problems closely to see if you should add or subtract. Circle the numbers. Underline the clues.

Example 1: Joey's dad baked muffins. On Saturday, he baked ⑧ muffins. On Sunday, he baked ⑩ muffins. How many muffins did he bake <u>all together</u>?

8 + 10 = 18

> The phrases *in all* and *in total* are other clues that you must add.

Example 2: Mrs. Parker had ⑮ erasers. She gave ⑦ of them to students. How many did she <u>have left</u>?

15 − 7 = 8

Your turn

① Solve each problem. Circle the numbers. Underline the clues. Draw pictures to help you solve it.

• Lin has ⑧ books. Luis has ⑥ books. How many books do they have <u>all together</u>?

 <u>8 + 6 = 14 books</u>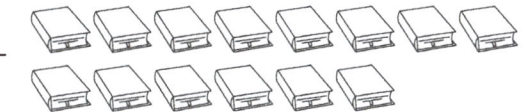

a Mr. Davis had 18 stickers. He passed out 10 stickers. How many stickers did he have left?

_____

SELF CHECK Mark how you feel

Got it! 😊 ☐   Need help... 😐 ☐   I don't get it 🙁 ☐

Check your answers
How many did you get correct? ☐

© Shell Education — 146444—Catch-Up Math — 23

WHOLE NUMBERS

Practice

1 Solve each problem. Circle the numbers. Underline the clues. Draw pictures to help you solve it.

• There are ⑥ black cats. There are ④ white cats. How many cats are there all together?

6 + 4 = 10 cats

a The birthday cake had 8 candles. Sara's mom added 4 more candles. How many total candles were on the cake?

_____

b Luis saw 14 soccer balls on the field. He kicked 7 balls down the field. How many soccer balls were left?

_____

c Max ate 3 pizza slices. James ate 4 pizza slices. How many did they eat in total?

_____

d Jessie held 4 marbles. Kevin held 7 marbles. How many marbles did they have in all?

_____

e Chloe went to the park. She met 10 dogs. Then, 3 of them walked away. How many were left?

_____

f Emma has 12 coins. She spends 3 of them. How many are left?

_____

WHOLE NUMBERS

2 Write the addition or subtraction equation for each problem.

● The bookshelf has 12 books. Then, 6 books are removed. How many books are left?

$\underline{\quad 12 - 6 = 6 \quad}$

a There are 8 paintbrushes on one table. There are 5 paintbrushes on another table. How many brushes are there all together?

_____

b One flower has 4 petals. Another flower has 7 petals. How many petals are there all together?

_____

c There are 14 airplanes at the airport. Then, 6 airplanes take off. How many are left?

_____

d Penny went to the zoo. She saw 9 monkeys. Then, 5 of them went inside to eat. How many were left?

_____

e Renee wanted 3 strawberries. She also wanted 5 blueberries. How many berries did she want in all?

_____

f Miguel had 7 playing cards. Robert had 7 playing cards. How many playing cards did they have in total?

_____

WHOLE NUMBERS

Two-Step Word Problems

Sometimes, you have to do two steps to solve a word problem.

Read two-step word problems closely. Circle the numbers, and underline the clues. Decide what steps you need to take to find the answer.

Example 1: Luis had ⓘ2 playing cards. Daniel had ⑧ playing cards. <u>Together</u>, they gave ④ cards to their friend Sasha. How many playing cards <u>were left</u>?

Step 1: 12 + 8 = <u>20</u>   Luis and Daniel had 20 cards all together.

Step 2: 20 − 4 = <u>16</u>   They had 16 cards left after they gave 4 to Sasha.

There were **16** playing cards left.

1 Read each word problem. Circle the numbers, and underline the clues. Write the equations for each step. Then, write the answer.

• There are ⑧ kids on the bus. At the first stop, ⑥ more kids get on the bus. At the next stop, ③ more kids get on the bus. How many kids are on the bus <u>in all</u>?

Step 1: _____ **8 + 6 = 14** _____

Step 2: _____ **14 + 3 = 17** _____

Answer: There are **17** kids on the bus in all.

a The coach had 12 soccer balls. Peter kicked 2 balls away. Juan kicked 4 balls away. How many were left?

Step 1: _____

Step 2: _____

Answer: There were _____ balls left.

SELF CHECK Mark how you feel
Got it!   Need help...   I don't get it

Check your answers
How many did you get correct?

Practice

WHOLE NUMBERS

1 Solve each two-step addition problem. Circle the numbers, and underline the clues. Write the equation for each step. Then, write the answer.

Nora had ②candies. Then, she got ④ more candies. Later, she got ③ more candies. How many candies did she have <u>in all</u>?

Step 1: _____2 + 4 = 6_____

Step 2: _____6 + 3 = 9_____

Answer: She had __9__ candies in all.

a James saw 4 birds in the sky. Then, 4 more birds flew by. Finally, 5 more birds flew by. How many birds did James see in all?

Step 1: _____

Step 2: _____

Answer: James saw _____ birds in all.

b Mr. Adams asked for 5 student helpers. Then, he needed 2 more helpers. Then, he asked for 6 more. How many helpers were there in all?

Step 1: _____

Step 2: _____

Answer: There were _____ helpers in all.

c The dog had 4 treats in the morning. It had 3 treats during the day. It had 6 treats at night. How many treats did the dog have in all?

Step 1: _____

Step 2: _____

Answer: The dog had _____ treats in all.

d Jade read 10 pages on Monday. She read 3 pages on Tuesday. She read 3 pages on Wednesday. How many pages did she read in all?

Step 1: _____

Step 2: _____

Answer: She read _____ pages in all.

WHOLE NUMBERS

2 Solve each two-step subtraction problem. Circle the numbers, and underline the clues. Write the equation for each step. Then, write the answer.

● Dante had ⑫ stickers. He put ③ stickers on his book. Then, he put ③ stickers on his desk. How many stickers <u>are left</u>?

Step 1: _____12 − 3 = 9_____

Step 2: _____9 − 3 = 6_____

Answer: There are __6__ stickers left.

a The store had 15 pairs of shoes. Jeff sold 4 pairs. Maria sold 6 pairs. How many pairs of shoes were left?

Step 1: _____

Step 2: _____

Answer: There were _____ pairs left.

b The bell rang at the end of the day. There were 16 kids in class. 4 kids went to the bus. 5 kids rode on their bikes. The rest of the class walked home. How many kids walked home?

Step 1: _____

Step 2: _____

Answer: _____ kids walked home.

c Sofia invited 10 kids to her party. 2 kids wore dresses. 3 kids wore skirts. The rest wore pants. How many kids wore pants?

Step 1: _____

Step 2: _____

Answer: _____ kids wore pants.

d Danny had 15 animal toys. There were 10 elephants. There were 3 lions. The rest were tigers. How many animal toys did Danny have?

Step 1: _____

Step 2: _____

Answer: Danny had _____ animal toys.

WHOLE NUMBERS

3 Solve each two-step problem. Circle the numbers, and underline the clues. Read closely. You may have to add and subtract. Write the equation for each step. Then, write the answer.

● The café baked ⑥ muffins and ④ cookies. Then, they sold ② cookies. How many treats <u>were left</u>?

Step 1: _____6 + 4 = 10_____

Step 2: _____10 − 2 = 8_____

Answer: There were __8__ treats left.

a Mrs. Lopez had 10 blue papers. She had 4 red papers. She passed out 2 red papers. How many papers were left?

Step 1: _____

Step 2: _____

Answer: There were _____ papers left.

b Jamal had 11 coins. Marco had 5 coins. They put their money together. Then, they spent 3 coins. How many coins were left?

Step 1: _____

Step 2: _____

Answer: There were _____ coins left.

c An artist painted 5 paintings last month. She painted 4 more paintings this month. Then, she sold 2 of them. How many paintings were left?

Step 1: _____

Step 2: _____

Answer: There were _____ paintings left.

d Jesse had 14 toy blocks. His brother gave him 3 more. Then, they used 6 blocks in a game. How many blocks were left?

Step 1: _____

Step 2: _____

Answer: There were _____ blocks left.

WHOLE NUMBERS

Expanded Form

Numbers can be written in expanded form. This form shows the value of each digit.

You can use base-ten blocks to show the expanded form of a number.

Example 1: In base-ten blocks, 154 would look like this:

Expanded Word Form: 1 hundred + 5 tens + 4 ones

Expanded Form: 100 + 50 + 4

Example 2: What is 238 in expanded word form and expanded form?

Expanded Word Form: 2 hundreds + 3 tens + 8 ones

Expanded Form: __200__ + __30__ + __8__

Example 3: What is the value of each digit?

⑧②⑥

The 8 is in the hundred place. So it is worth 800.

The 2 is in the tens place. So it is worth 20.

The 6 is in the ones place. So it is worth 6.

SCAN to watch video

Your turn

1 Write each number in expanded form.

● 582 = __500__ + __80__ + __2__

a 369 = _____ + _____ + _____

b 453 = _____ + _____ + _____

c 712 = _____ + _____ + _____

2 Write the value of each underlined digit.

● 6̲38 = __600__

a 24̲5 = _____   b 167̲ = _____   c 3̲15 = _____

SELF CHECK Mark how you feel

Got it! ☐   Need help... ☐   I don't get it  ☐

Check your answers
How many did you get correct?

Practice

WHOLE NUMBERS

1 Write each amount in expanded word form.

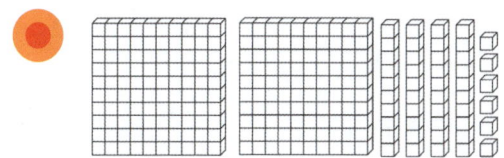

⎯⎯**2**⎯⎯ hundreds + ⎯⎯**4**⎯⎯ tens + ⎯⎯**6**⎯⎯ ones

a

⎯⎯⎯⎯ hundreds + ⎯⎯⎯⎯ ten + ⎯⎯⎯⎯ ones

b

⎯⎯⎯⎯ hundreds + ⎯⎯⎯⎯ tens + ⎯⎯⎯⎯ ones

c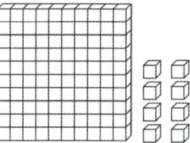

⎯⎯⎯⎯ hundred + ⎯⎯⎯⎯ tens + ⎯⎯⎯⎯ ones

2 Write each number in standard form.

● 5 hundreds + 6 tens + 3 ones = ⎯⎯**563**⎯⎯

a 4 hundreds + 3 tens + 2 ones = ⎯⎯⎯⎯

b 2 hundreds + 6 tens + 1 one = ⎯⎯⎯⎯

c 1 hundred + 8 tens + 7 ones = ⎯⎯⎯⎯

d 2 hundreds + 5 tens + 6 ones = ⎯⎯⎯⎯

WHOLE NUMBERS

3 Write the value of each underlined digit.

● 2<u>6</u>6   **60**

a 32<u>5</u> _____

b <u>4</u>98 _____

c 5<u>6</u>1 _____

d 4<u>3</u>0 _____

e 21<u>7</u> _____

4 Complete the tasks.

● Circle the digits that have a value of 50.

35, ⑤9, 175, 1⑤6, 3⑤7

a Circle the digits that have a value of 800.

890, 680, 812, 348, 788

b Circle the digits that have a value of 6.

26, 761, 846, 165, 966

c Circle the digits that have a value of 70.

76, 47, 275, 763, 277

5 Write each number in expanded form.

● 278 = __**200 + 70 + 8**__

a 426 = _____

b 835 = _____

c 180 = _____

d 592 = _____

e 844 = _____

f 350 = _____

g 961 = _____

h 718 = _____

i 219 = _____

WHOLE NUMBERS

Order Numbers

Numbers can be put in order from largest to smallest or from smallest to largest.

Example 1: Order the numbers from smallest to largest.

Look at the hundreds place first.

210, 376, 255

Then, look at the tens place.

Look at the ones place, if needed.

The correct order is **210, 255, 376**.

Cross out a number from the list once you have used it. This will help you stay organized.

Example 2: Order the numbers from largest to smallest.

518, 298, 581

Follow the same steps, but look for the larger numbers. Start in the hundreds place. Then, look at the tens place. Then, look at the ones place, if needed.

The correct order is **581, 518, 298**.

Your turn

1 Put the numbers in order from smallest to largest.

• 37, 85, 64

37, 64, 85

a 53, 12, 76

_____

b 144, 262, 118

_____

2 Put the numbers in order from largest to smallest.

• 124, 355, 138

355, 138, 124

a 973, 210, 458

_____

b 232, 323, 133

_____

SELF CHECK Mark how you feel

Got it! ☐   Need help...  ☐   I don't get it  ☐

Check your answers
How many did you get correct?

WHOLE NUMBERS

Practice

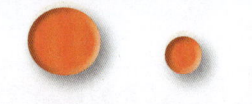

1 Write each set of numbers in order from smallest to largest.

● 28, 81, 47

28, 47, 81

a 89, 81, 18

_____

b 45, 24, 52

_____

c 76, 97, 91

_____

d 303, 110, 235

_____

e 95, 204, 105, 244, 501

_____

f 487, 655, 294, 578, 566

_____

g 184, 193, 195, 176, 299

_____

2 Write each set of numbers in order from largest to smallest.

● 43, 27, 59

59, 43, 27

a 37, 27, 56

_____

b 77, 33, 65

_____

c 36, 29, 68

_____

d 232, 323, 133

_____

e 600, 800, 400, 599, 782

_____

f 485, 685, 785, 825, 681

_____

g 509, 513, 570, 601, 489

_____

Whole Numbers Review

1 Complete the chart.

	Base-Ten Blocks	Standard Form	Words
a		26	twenty-six
b			thirty-five
c		62	
d			
e		55	
f			thirteen

2 Write the missing numbers in each set. You will need to count by twos, fives, tens, 25s, or 100s.

a 100, 200, _____, 400, _____, _____

b 2, 4, _____, _____, 10, 12

c 20, 30, 40, _____, 60, _____

d 50, 75, _____, _____, _____, 175

e 35, 40, _____, _____, 55, 60

WHOLE NUMBERS

Review

3 Write each set of numbers in order from smallest to largest.

  a 65, 75, 68, 88, 78

  _____

  b 754, 596, 291, 750, 511

  _____

  c 45, 113, 99, 32, 139

  _____

4 Write each set of numbers in order from largest to smallest.

  a 97, 257, 115, 322, 511

  _____

  b 478, 677, 294, 578, 588

  _____

  c 167, 193, 195, 178, 399

  _____

5 Solve the word problems. Draw pictures or write equations to help you.

  a Addy has 12 stuffed dogs and 4 stuffed cats. How many stuffed animals does she have in all?

  She has _____ stuffed animals.

  b Solomon had 20 markers. He gave 10 to his brother. Then, he gave 3 to his sister. How many markers did he have left?

  He had _____ markers left.

Review

WHOLE NUMBERS

6 Write each number in expanded form.

a 387 = _____

b 435 = _____

c 673 = _____

d 875 = _____

e 112 = _____

7 Write each number in standard form.

a 600 + 40 + 1 = _____   d 3 + 90 + 500 = _____

b 200 + 60 + 8 = _____   e 400 + 70 + 3 = _____

c 50 + 400 + 7 = _____   f 200 + 5 = _____

8 Write each number in word form.

a 187 = _____

b 935 = _____

c 712 = _____

d 254 = _____

e 356 = _____

MENTAL MATH

Fact Families to 20

A fact family uses the same three numbers to build addition and subtraction equations.

A fact family includes 2 addition and 2 subtraction equations. The same 3 numbers are used for all 4 equations.

Example 1: 3, 4, and 7 are a fact family.

3 + 4 = 7
4 + 3 = 7
7 − 4 = 3
7 − 3 = 4

Example 2: 3, 6, and 9 are a fact family.

3 + 6 = 9
6 + 3 = 9
9 − 6 = 3
9 − 3 = 6

Your turn

1. Use the numbers to write equations for each fact family.

• 4, 5, and 9

__5__ + __4__ = __9__
__4__ + __5__ = __9__
__9__ − __4__ = __5__
__9__ − __5__ = __4__

a 3, 5, and 8

____ + ____ = ____
____ + ____ = ____
____ − ____ = ____
____ − ____ = ____

Learning a fact family helps you quickly learn 4 math facts!

SELF CHECK Mark how you feel
Got it! | Need help... | I don't get it

Check your answers
How many did you get correct?

Practice

MENTAL MATH

1 Complete the equations for each fact family.

● 5 + __6__ = 11

6 + 5 = __11__

11 − __6__ = 5

11 − __5__ = 6

b 8 + 2 = _____

2 + _____ = 10

10 − 2 = _____

10 − _____ = 2

d 7 + 6 = _____

6 + _____ = 13

13 − 7 = _____

13 − _____ = 7

a 6 + 8 = _____

8 + _____ = 14

14 − 6 = _____

14 − _____ = 6

c 7 + 4 = _____

4 + _____ = 11

11 − 4 = _____

11 − _____ = 4

e 8 + 3 = _____

_____ + 8 = 11

11 − 3 = _____

11 − _____ = 3

2 Use the numbers to write equations for each fact family.

● 6, 9, 15

__6__ + __9__ = __15__

__9__ + __6__ = __15__

__15__ − __6__ = __9__

__15__ − __9__ = __6__

b 3, 8, 11

___ + ___ = ___

___ + ___ = ___

___ − ___ = ___

___ − ___ = ___

d 3, 7, 10

___ + ___ = ___

___ + ___ = ___

___ − ___ = ___

___ − ___ = ___

a 5, 7, 12

___ + ___ = ___

___ + ___ = ___

___ − ___ = ___

___ − ___ = ___

c 2, 6, 8

___ + ___ = ___

___ + ___ = ___

___ − ___ = ___

___ − ___ = ___

e 4, 6, 10

___ + ___ = ___

___ + ___ = ___

___ − ___ = ___

___ − ___ = ___

MENTAL MATH

Count On

You can count on to add. Start with the larger number. Then, add the smaller number.

Example 1: Use a number line to solve 4 + 8.

Start with 8. Add 4.

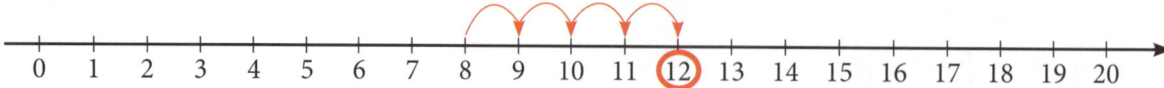

4 + 8 = __12__

Example 2: Count on with your fingers to add 7 + 4. Start with 7. Count on 4 more.

 7 + 4 = __11__

> Why is it better to start with the larger number and not the smaller number?

 **Your turn**

1 Count on to find each answer. Show your work on the number lines.

● 5 + 3 = __8__

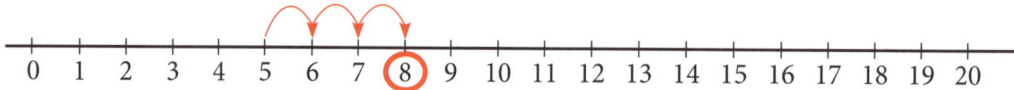

a 5 + 7 = _____

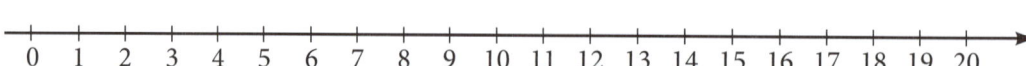

SELF CHECK Mark how you feel

Got it!  ☐   Need help...  ☐   I don't get it ☐

Check your answers How many did you get correct?

Practice

MENTAL MATH

1 Count on to find each answer. Show your work on the number lines.

● $6 + 3 = \underline{9}$

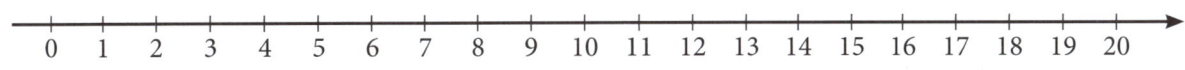

a $9 + 4 = \underline{}$

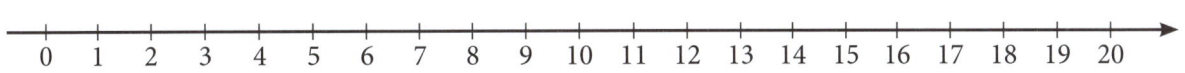

b $7 + 2 = \underline{}$

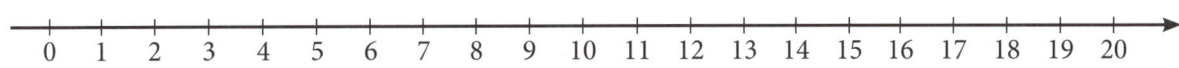

c $6 + 8 = \underline{}$

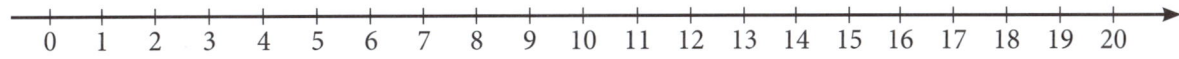

d $9 + 2 = \underline{}$

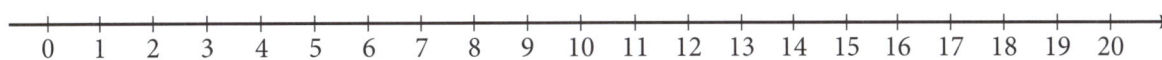

e $5 + 13 = \underline{}$

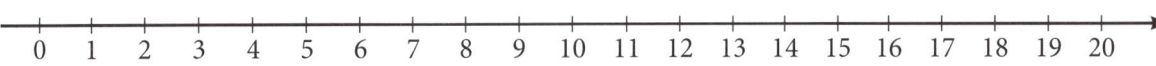

f $15 + 4 = \underline{}$

g $3 + 17 = \underline{}$

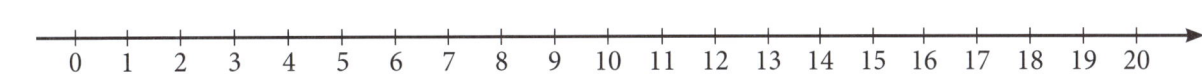

MENTAL MATH

2 Count on with your fingers. Remember to start with the larger number.

● 7 + 3 = __10__

a 2 + 8 = _____

b 1 + 8 = _____

c 8 + 5 = _____

d 9 + 6 = _____

e 2 + 11 = _____

f 9 + 4 = _____

g 7 + 6 = _____

3 Now try bigger numbers. Count on with your fingers.

● 19 + 3 = [22]

a 17 + 2 = [ ]

b 3 + 22 = [ ]

c 2 + 26 = [ ]

d 14 + 3 = [ ]

e 18 + 3 = [ ]

f 21 + 5 = [ ]

g 19 + 7 = [ ]

4 Use mental math. Count on in your head.

● 5 + 11 = (16)

a 8 + 6 = ( )

b 5 + 9 = ( )

c 7 + 3 = ( )

d 24 + 5 = ( )

e 4 + 19 = ( )

f 22 + 2 = ( )

g 4 + 23 = ( )

MENTAL MATH

Count Back

You can count back to subtract one number from another.

To count back, start with the larger number. Then, count back the smaller number.

Example 1: Count back with a number line to solve 9 − 3.

Start with 9. Count back 3.

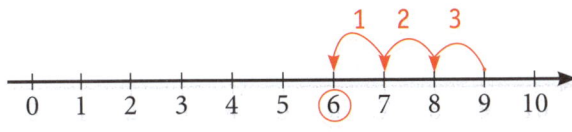

9 − 3 = __6__

Example 2: Count back with your fingers to solve 12 − 5.

Start by saying "12." Count back as you put up each finger. Stop when you have 5 fingers up.

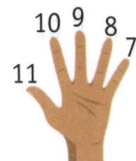

12 − 5 = __7__

Your turn

1 Count back to find each answer. Show your work on the number line.

● 8 − 5 = __3__

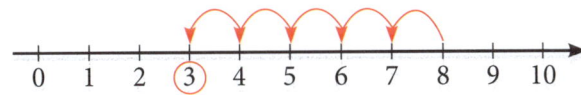

a 7 − 4 = _____

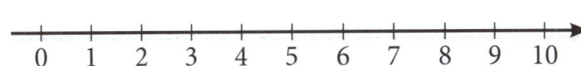

"You can also count back in your head. Give it a try!"

SELF CHECK Mark how you feel
- Got it!
- Need help...
- I don't get it

Check your answers
How many did you get correct?

MENTAL MATH

Practice

1 Count back to find each answer. Show your work on the number lines.

• 10 − 3 = **7**

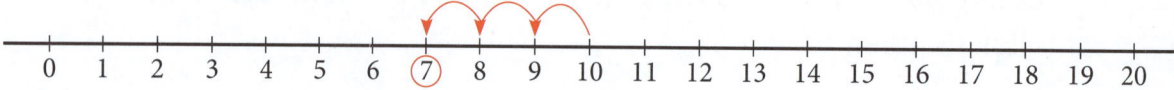

a   13 − 4 = _____

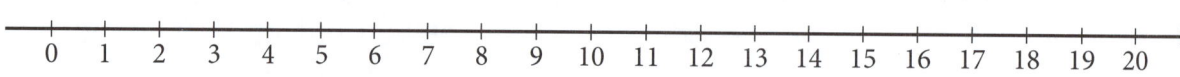

b   9 − 2 = _____

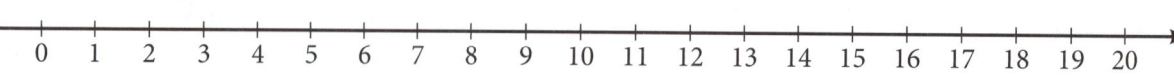

c   15 − 6 = _____

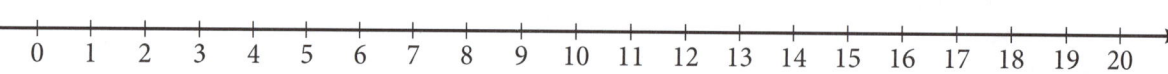

d   17 − 5 = _____

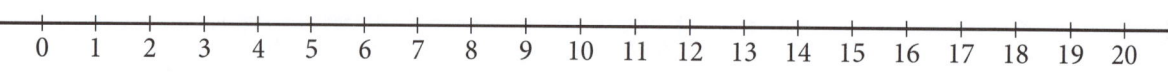

e   19 − 6 = _____

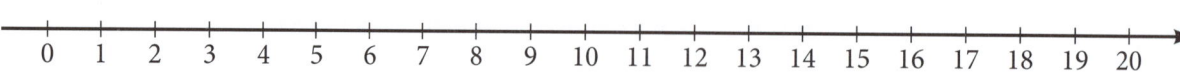

f   8 − 3 = _____

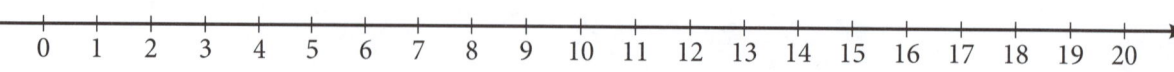

g   15 − 7 = _____

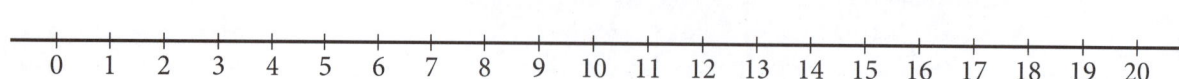

MENTAL MATH

Make Tens

You can make a 10 to solve an addition problem.

Example 1: 8 + 4 = ?

8 + 4 = 12
   / \
  2   2

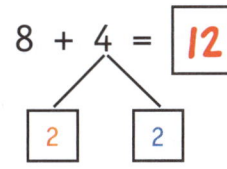

You can split the 4 into 2 and 2 because you know 8 + 2 makes 10.

Think $\begin{cases} 8 + 2 = 10 \\ 10 + 2 = 12 \end{cases}$

Your turn

1 Solve each problem by making a 10. Write numbers in the boxes to show your thinking.

● 9 + 4 = __13__
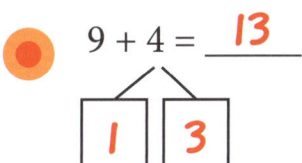
   1   3

a 7 + 5 = _____

b 8 + 3 = _____

SELF CHECK Mark how you feel
Got it!   Need help...   I don't get it

Check your answers
How many did you get correct?

MENTAL MATH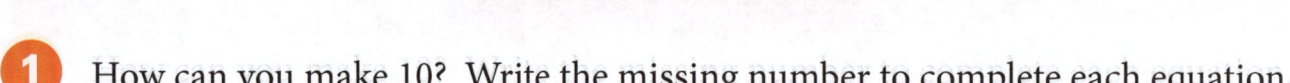

Practice

1 How can you make 10? Write the missing number to complete each equation.

● __10__ + 0 = 10   e _____ + 5 = 10

a _____ + 1 = 10   f _____ + 6 = 10

b _____ + 2 = 10   g _____ + 7 = 10

c _____ + 3 = 10   h _____ + 8 = 10

d _____ + 4 = 10   i _____ + 9 = 10

2 What patterns do you notice above?

_____

_____

_____

3 Write the missing number to make each equation true.

● __7__ + 3 = 10   d 8 + _____ = 10

a 5 + _____ = 10   e _____ + 7 = 10

b _____ + 4 = 10   f 0 + _____ = 10

c 1 + _____ = 10   g _____ + 2 = 10

46   146444—Catch-Up Math   © Shell Education

MENTAL MATH

4 Solve each problem by making a 10. Write numbers in the boxes to show your thinking.

● 8 + 6 = __14__
    | 2 | 4 |

e 9 + 8 = ____

a 7 + 4 = ____

f 6 + 7 = ____

b 8 + 5 = ____

g 7 + 5 = ____

c 6 + 9 = ____

h 9 + 5 = ____

d 6 + 6 = ____

i 8 + 8 = ____

MENTAL MATH

Doubles + or − 1

A double is adding two numbers that are the same, such as 4 + 4. You can use doubles facts to quickly add doubles plus or minus 1.

If you know 5 + 5, you can also learn 4 + 5 and 6 + 5.

   5 + 5 = __10__

   5 + 4 is the same as 5 + 5 − 1. They both equal 9.

   5 + 6 is the same as 5 + 5 + 1. They both equal 11.

Know Your Doubles Facts

| 1 + 1 = 2 | 3 + 3 = 6 | 5 + 5 = 10 | 7 + 7 = 14 | 9 + 9 = 18 |
| 2 + 2 = 4 | 4 + 4 = 8 | 6 + 6 = 12 | 8 + 8 = 16 | 10 + 10 = 20 |

1 Solve these doubles plus 1 problems.

• 6 + 7 = ?

    6 + 6 + 1 = __13__

b 7 + 8 = ?

    7 + 7 + 1 = _____

a 4 + 5 = ?

    4 + 4 + 1 = _____

c 8 + 9 = ?

    8 + 8 + 1 = _____

SELF CHECK Mark how you feel

Got it! Need help... I don't get it

Check your answers
How many did you get correct?

Practice

MENTAL MATH

1 Solve each doubles problem.

- 5 + 5 = __10__
- a 1 + 1 = _____
- b 3 + 3 = _____
- c 8 + 8 = _____
- d 2 + 2 = _____
- e 11 + 11 = _____
- f 7 + 7 = _____
- g 4 + 4 = _____
- h 6 + 6 = _____
- i 10 + 10 = _____

2 Solve each doubles fact. Then, solve the related math facts.

- 4 + 4 = __8__
  4 + 5 = ?
  4 + 4 + 1 = __9__
  4 + 3 = ?
  4 + 4 − 1 = __7__

- b 3 + 3 = _____
  4 + 3 = ?
  3 + 3 + 1 = _____
  2 + 3 = ?
  3 + 3 − 1 = _____

- d 2 + 2 = _____
  3 + 2 = ?
  2 + 2 + 1 = _____
  1 + 2 = ?
  2 + 2 − 1 = _____

- a 5 + 5 = _____
  6 + 5 = ?
  5 + 5 + 1 = _____
  4 + 5 = ?
  5 + 5 − 1 = _____

- c 8 + 8 = _____
  9 + 8 = ?
  8 + 8 + 1 = _____
  7 + 8 = ?
  8 + 8 − 1 = _____

- e 11 + 11 = _____
  12 + 11 = ?
  11 + 11 + 1 = _____
  10 + 11 = ?
  11 + 11 − 1 = _____

MENTAL MATH

Commutative Property

You can add numbers in any order and get the same answer. This is called the *Commutative Property*.

Example 1: If you know that 4 + 8 = 12…

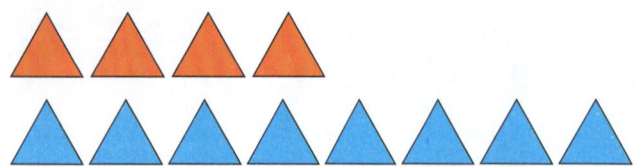

then, you know that 8 + 4 = 12.

The Commutative Property does **not** work for subtraction.

Example 2: This is also true if you add three numbers together. You can add them in any order. You will always get the same answer!

4 + 5 + 2 = 11 and 5 + 2 + 4 = 11 and 2 + 4 + 5 = 11

Your turn

1 Solve each problem.

●   9 + 8 = __17__   8 + 9 = __17__

a   4 + 8 = _____   8 + 4 = _____

b   8 + 5 = _____   5 + 8 = _____

c   5 + 9 = _____   9 + 5 = _____

d   6 + 7 = _____   7 + 6 = _____

Check your answers
How many did you get correct?

Practice

MENTAL MATH

1 Write the missing number to make each equation true.

● __4__ + 5 = 9

5 + __4__ = 9

b 4 + ____ = 10

6 + ____ = 10

d 7 + ____ = 12

____ + ____ = 12

a 3 + ____ = 11

8 + ____ = 11

c 5 + ____ = 9

4 + ____ = 9

e 8 + ____ = 14

____ + ____ = 14

2 Write the missing number to make each equation true.

● 4 + 2 + __5__ = 11

5 + 4 + __2__ = 11

b 4 + ____ + 3 = 12

5 + ____ + 4 = 12

d ____ + 7 + 3 = 16

____ + 6 + 7 = 16

a 6 + 4 + ____ = 12

2 + 6 + ____ = 12

c 6 + ____ + 5 = 15

4 + ____ + 6 = 15

e ____ + 8 + 2 = 13

____ + 3 + 2 = 13

3 Write three addition equations with the same numbers. Switch the order of the numbers for each equation.

● __7__ + __4__ + __3__ = __14__

__3__ + __7__ + __4__ = __14__

__4__ + __7__ + __3__ = __14__

a ___ + ___ + ___ = ___

___ + ___ + ___ = ___

___ + ___ + ___ = ___

MENTAL MATH

Addition Facts to 20

Knowing addition facts to 20 will help you solve many kinds of math problems quickly.

There are different ways to solve addition facts within 20. Some include:

- using fact families
- counting on
- making a 10
- learning doubles
- knowing the commutative property

 Test yourself. See how quickly you can solve these math facts.

a $5 + 3 = $ _____   f $6 + 6 = $ _____

b $4 + 2 = $ _____   g $2 + 9 = $ _____

c $0 + 6 = $ _____   h $4 + 5 = $ _____

d $1 + 7 = $ _____   i $6 + 2 = $ _____

e $8 + 4 = $ _____   j $3 + 5 = $ _____

Which mental math strategies do you prefer?

SELF CHECK   Mark how you feel

Got it!  ☐   Need help... ☐   I don't get it ☐

Check your answers
How many did you get correct?

Practice

MENTAL MATH

1 Write the missing numbers in the addition chart. Some numbers have been added for you.

+	1	2	3	4	5	6	7	8	9	10
1	2				6	7				
2								10		
3		5						11		13
4				8			11		13	
5		7	8	9			12		14	15
6	7			10				14		
7		9								
8			11		13		15		17	18
9				13		16	17			19
10				14				18	19	

2 What patterns do you notice in the addition chart?

_____

_____

_____

_____

MENTAL MATH

3 Solve the problems. Use any strategy.

a   3 + 3 = _____   h   5 + 5 = _____   o   8 + 2 = _____

b   4 + 5 = _____   i   6 + 4 = _____   p   1 + 2 = _____

c   6 + 2 = _____   j   1 + 4 = _____   q   4 + 3 = _____

d   8 + 0 = _____   k   2 + 5 = _____   r   2 + 7 = _____

e   5 + 1 = _____   l   7 + 7 = _____   s   9 + 6 = _____

f   4 + 7 = _____   m   0 + 3 = _____   t   3 + 9 = _____

g   3 + 7 = _____   n   7 + 3 = _____   u   8 + 9 = _____

4 Circle the strategies you used to solve these problems.

fact families   making a 10   commutative property

counting on   using doubles

5 Which strategies worked best for you? Why?

_____

_____

_____

MENTAL MATH

Subtraction Facts to 20

Knowing subtraction facts to 20 will help you solve many kinds of math problems quickly.

There are different ways to solve subtraction facts within 20. Some include:

- using fact families
- counting back on your fingers
- learning doubles

1 Test yourself. See how quickly you can solve these math facts.

a 8 − 6 = ____

b 6 − 2 = ____

c 10 − 5 = ____

d 8 − 1 = ____

e 12 − 4 = ____

f 14 − 4 = ____

g 11 − 2 = ____

h 9 − 3 = ____

i 7 − 5 = ____

j 12 − 10 = ____

Which mental math strategies do you prefer? Do you know any others?

SELF CHECK Mark how you feel

Got it!   Need help...   I don't get it

Check your answers
How many did you get correct?

MENTAL MATH

Practice

1 Solve the problems. Use any strategy.

a 6 – 3 = ____   h 11 – 5 = ____   o 7 – 3 = ____

b 16 – 6 = ____   i 8 – 4 = ____   p 10 – 7 = ____

c 8 – 2 = ____   j 14 – 4 = ____   q 12 – 6 = ____

d 10 – 3 = ____   k 9 – 2 = ____   r 16 – 8 = ____

e 5 – 1 = ____   l 10 – 5 = ____   s 15 – 6 = ____

f 12 – 3 = ____   m 3 – 2 = ____   t 13 – 5 = ____

g 19 – 8 = ____   n 20 – 5 = ____   u 17 – 8 = ____

2 Circle the strategies you used to solve these problems.

fact families   counting back   using doubles

3 Which strategies worked best for you? Why?

_____

_____

_____

Mental Math Review

1 Write four equations for each fact family.

a 5, 8, 13

___ + ___ = ___

___ + ___ = ___

___ − ___ = ___

___ − ___ = ___

c 8, 6, 14

___ + ___ = ___

___ + ___ = ___

___ − ___ = ___

___ − ___ = ___

b 3, 6, 9

___ + ___ = ___

___ + ___ = ___

___ − ___ = ___

___ − ___ = ___

d 5, 10, 15

___ + ___ = ___

___ + ___ = ___

___ − ___ = ___

___ − ___ = ___

2 Write the missing numbers in each fact family.

a 9 + 6 = ___

6 + ___ = 15

15 − 9 = ___

15 − ___ = 9

c 1 + 9 = ___

9 + ___ = 10

10 − 1 = ___

10 − ___ = 1

b 5 + 3 = ___

3 + ___ = 8

8 − 3 = ___

8 − ___ = 3

d 5 + 9 = ___

9 + ___ = 14

14 − 5 = ___

14 − ___ = 5

MENTAL MATH

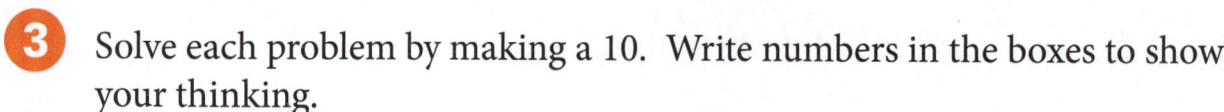

3 Solve each problem by making a 10. Write numbers in the boxes to show your thinking.

a 8 + 3 = _____

b 9 + 5 = _____

c 6 + 8 = _____

d 7 + 8 = _____

e 9 + 9 = _____

f 7 + 7 = _____

4 Write the missing numbers to make the equations true.

a 6 + 5 = 11

5 + _____ = 11

b 3 + 7 = 10

7 + _____ = 10

c 5 + _____ = 12

7 + _____ = 12

d 3 + _____ = 9

6 + _____ = 9

e 9 + _____ = 12

3 + _____ = 12

f 6 + _____ = 14

8 + _____ = 14

Review

MENTAL MATH

5 Write the missing number to make each equation true.

a   4 + 3 + 2 = 9

     2 + 3 + _____ = 9

b   6 + 5 + 3 = 14

     3 + 6 + _____ = 14

c   5 + _____ + 6 = 15

     5 + _____ + 4 = 15

d   7 + _____ + 5 = 20

     5 + _____ + 8 = 20

e   _____ + 7 + 3 = 18

     _____ + 8 + 7 = 18

f   _____ + 8 + 9 = 19

     _____ + 8 + 2 = 19

6 Use the Commutative Property. Create pairs of equations with the same sums.

a   _____ + _____ = 9

     _____ + _____ = 9

b   _____ + _____ = 12

     _____ + _____ = 12

c   _____ + _____ + _____ = 18

     _____ + _____ + _____ = 18

MENTAL MATH

Review

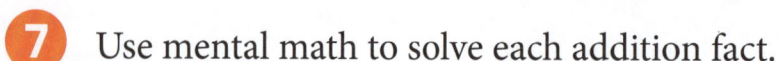

7 Use mental math to solve each addition fact.

- **a** 4 + 5 = _____
- **b** 6 + 2 = _____
- **c** 5 + 7 = _____
- **d** 11 + 7 = _____
- **e** 6 + 8 = _____
- **f** 3 + 3 = _____
- **g** 13 + 4 = _____
- **h** 10 + 5 = _____
- **i** 4 + 6 = _____
- **j** 5 + 1 = _____
- **k** 8 + 0 = _____
- **l** 1 + 12 = _____
- **m** 17 + 3 = _____
- **n** 8 + 9 = _____
- **o** 11 + 5 = _____

8 Use mental math to solve each subtraction fact.

- **a** 6 − 3 = _____
- **b** 10 − 8 = _____
- **c** 17 − 1 = _____
- **d** 19 − 8 = _____
- **e** 16 − 6 = _____
- **f** 10 − 3 = _____
- **g** 5 − 1 = _____
- **h** 10 − 5 = _____
- **i** 12 − 3 = _____
- **j** 3 − 2 = _____
- **k** 11 − 5 = _____
- **l** 8 − 2 = _____
- **m** 14 − 4 = _____
- **n** 9 − 2 = _____
- **o** 18 − 6 = _____

PLACE VALUE

Tens and Ones

Place value is the value of a digit based on where it is in a number.

A 2-digit number has a digit in the ones place and a digit in the tens place.

tens place ←—68—→ ones place

In the number 68, the 6 equals 60, and the 8 equals 8.

Example 1: The number 57 is made up of 5 tens and 7 ones. If you build 57 with base-ten blocks, it will look like this:

Example 2: How many tens and ones are in 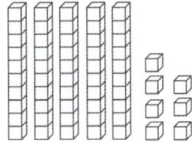?

There are 7 tens.

There are 2 ones.

1 Write how many tens and ones are in each number.

- 39 __3__ tens __9__ ones

a 46 _____ tens _____ ones

b 52 _____ tens _____ ones

c 17 _____ ten _____ ones

d 93 _____ tens _____ ones

SELF CHECK Mark how you feel
Got it!   Need help...   I don't get it

Check your answers
How many did you get correct?

© Shell Education   146444—Catch-Up Math   61

PLACE VALUE

Practice

1 Color the tens and ones to match each number.

	Number	Tens	Ones
•	62		
a	41		
b	72		
c	58		
d	30		
e	17		
f	67		
g	81		

PLACE VALUE

2 Write each number in expanded form. Then, draw the number with base-ten blocks. Use lines for tens and dots for ones.

 42 = __4__ tens __2__ ones

42 = __40__ + __2__

a 63 = _____ tens _____ ones

63 = _____ + _____

b 37 = _____ tens _____ ones

37 = _____ + _____

c 81 = _____ tens _____ one

81 = _____ + _____

d 16 = _____ ten _____ ones

16 = _____ + _____

e 25 = _____ tens _____ ones

25 = _____ + _____

f 72 = _____ tens _____ ones

72 = _____ + _____

PLACE VALUE

Greater Than, Less Than, Equal To

You can use place value to compare the values of numbers.

Use these symbols to compare numbers:

greater than   >

less than   <

equal to   =

Example 1: 25 > 16 means 25 is greater than 16.

24 = 24 means 24 is equal to 24.

39 < 50 means 39 is less than 50.

Example 2: Look at the largest place value first. If they are the same, look at the next largest place value. You can compare 20 and 25. They both have a 2 in the tens place, so look at the ones place. Since 5 is greater than 0, then…

20 < 25

Your turn

1 Write *True* or *False* for each comparison.

● 15 > 25 ___False___

a 71 = 71 _____

b 50 > 51 _____

c 24 < 42 _____

d 11 = 10 _____

e 73 > 70 _____

The open side of the < and > symbols always face the larger number.

SELF CHECK — Mark how you feel

Got it!   Need help…   I don't get it

Check your answers — How many did you get correct?

64   146444—Catch-Up Math   © Shell Education

Practice

PLACE VALUE

1 Complete each comparison. Use the words *greater than*, *less than*, or *equal to*.

● 32 is __less than__ 35   d 53 is _____ 58

a 42 is _____ 42   e 16 is _____ 16

b 24 is _____ 54   f 20 is _____ 50

c 76 is _____ 67   g 70 is _____ 50

2 Write <, >, or = to make each comparison true.

● 67 < 76   d 64 ◯ 65

a 55 ◯ 66   e 15 ◯ 11

b 37 ◯ 37   f 20 ◯ 30

c 28 ◯ 82   g 25 ◯ 25

3 Circle the numbers that fit each rule.

● greater than 20   c greater than 53

   (24), 15, (72), 2   54, 57, 35, 50

a less than 50   d less than 66

   44, 51, 49, 5   60, 66, 68, 6

b equal to 37   e greater than 80

   33, 73, 77, 37   81, 78, 77, 85

PLACE VALUE

4 Write a number that could make each comparison true. There is more than one right answer.

🔴 35 < __48__ < 55

a   40 < _____ < 60

b   20 < _____ < 80

c   36 < _____ < 86

d   22 < _____ < 26

e   78 < _____ < 88

f   39 < _____ < 50

g   52 < _____ < 55

h   50 < _____ < 60

i   11 < _____ < 22

j   39 < _____ < 49

k   44 > _____ > 40

l   82 > _____ > 78

m   25 > _____ > 20

n   15 > _____ > 6

o   67 > _____ > 57

p   42 > _____ > 32

q   44 > _____ > 40

r   62 > _____ > 45

s   99 > _____ > 87

5 Write two numbers that could make each comparison true. There are many right answers.

🔴 ? > 15

__17__ __28__

a   ? > 45

_____ _____

b   ? < 32

_____ _____

c   ? < 16

_____ _____

d   ? > 73

_____ _____

e   ? > 85

_____ _____

PLACE VALUE

Compare Three-Digit Numbers

You can compare three-digit numbers. Three-digit numbers have digits in the hundreds place, tens place, and ones place.

Example 1: 150 > 100 means 150 is greater than 100.

245 = 245 means 245 is equal to 245.

672 < 740 means 672 is less than 740.

Example 2: 4<u>3</u>9 (?) 4<u>9</u>3

Look at the hundreds place first. Both numbers have a 4 in the hundreds place. So, look at the digits in the tens place next. Since 9 is greater than 3, the number with the 9 in the tens place is bigger.

439 < 493

The open side of the < or > symbol should always open toward the larger number.

Your turn

1 Circle the correct term to complete each comparison.

● 40 is greater than / (less than) / equal to 150

a   225 is greater than / less than / equal to 222

b   345 is greater than / less than / equal to 543

c   141 is greater than / less than / equal to 141

d   609 is greater than / less than / equal to 610

If the digits in the hundreds place and the tens place are the same, compare the numbers in the ones place.

SELF CHECK Mark how you feel
Got it!   Need help...   I don't get it

Check your answers
How many did you get correct?

© Shell Education

146444—Catch-Up Math

67

PLACE VALUE

1 Write *True* or *False* for each comparison.

● 213 > 230 __False__

a 860 > 814 _____

b 420 < 402 _____

c 589 < 895 _____

d 370 = 370 _____

e 109 > 110 _____

f 442 > 424 _____

g 199 < 188 _____

2 Circle the numbers that fit each rule.

● greater than 125

(126), 100, (215)

a greater than 150

126, 200, 215

b less than 240

204, 200, 294

c greater than 389

390, 400, 309

d less than 209

200, 201, 210

e less than 444

400, 500, 600

3 Write two numbers that could make each comparison true. There are many right answers.

● 240 > ?

__230__ __220__

a 134 > ?

_____ _____

b ? > 356

_____ _____

c 570 > ?

_____ _____

d ? > 250

_____ _____

e 220 > ?

_____ _____

68 146444—Catch-Up Math © Shell Education

PLACE VALUE

4 Complete each comparison. Use the words *greater than*, *less than*, or *equal to*.

● 135 is __less than__ 235   d 244 is _____ 220

a 340 is _____ 440   e 700 is _____ 850

b 200 is _____ 500   f 900 is _____ 899

c 150 is _____ 150   g 325 is _____ 315

5 Write <, >, or = to make each comparison true.

● 380 **<** 400   d 476 ◯ 450

a 200 ◯ 210   e 135 ◯ 135

b 315 ◯ 130   f 789 ◯ 987

c 879 ◯ 879   g 308 ◯ 380

6 Write a number that could make each comparison true. There is more than one right answer.

● 35 < __48__ < 55   e 324 < _____ < 423

a 403 < _____ < 680   f 981 < _____ < 985

b 196 < _____ < 380   g 432 < _____ < 544

c 101 < _____ < 976   h 639 < _____ < 641

d 111 < _____ < 185   i 291 < _____ < 297

PLACE VALUE

10 More and 10 Less

You can use place-value patterns to find 10 more or 10 less than a number.

Example 1: Find 10 more by adding 10 to a number.

$$10 + 10 = 20$$
$$20 + 10 = 30$$
$$30 + 10 = 40$$

Pattern: Only the digit in the tens place changes. It goes up by 1.

$$34 + 10 = 44$$
$$44 + 10 = \underline{\,54\,}$$
$$54 + 10 = \underline{\,64\,}$$

Example 2: Find 10 less by subtracting 10 from a number.

$$50 - 10 = 40$$
$$40 - 10 = 30$$
$$30 - 10 = 20$$

Pattern: Only the digit in the tens place changes. It goes down by 1.

$$57 - 10 = 47$$
$$47 - 10 = \underline{\,37\,}$$
$$37 - 10 = \underline{\,27\,}$$

Example 3: You can use a hundred chart. Move down one row to add 10. Move up one row to subtract 10.

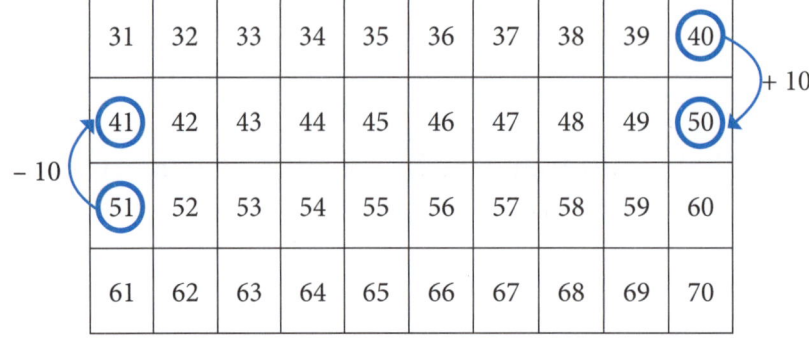

Your turn

1 Solve each problem.

● $48 + 10 = \underline{\,58\,}$

a $76 + 10 = \underline{}$

b $24 + 10 = \underline{}$

When you add or subtract 10, the ones place will stay the same!

SELF CHECK   Mark how you feel

| Got it!  | Need help...  ☐ | I don't get it  ☐ |

Check your answers
How many did you get correct? ☐

Practice

PLACE VALUE

1 Use the hundred chart to add.

1	2	3	4	5	6	7	8	9	10
11	12	13	14	15	16	17	18	19	20
21	22	23	24	25	26	27	28	29	30
31	32	33	34	35	36	37	38	39	40
41	42	43	44	45	46	47	48	49	50
51	52	53	54	55	56	57	58	59	60
61	62	63	64	65	66	67	68	69	70
71	72	73	74	75	76	77	78	79	80
81	82	83	84	85	86	87	88	89	90
91	92	93	94	95	96	97	98	99	100

● 54 + 10 = **64**

a 32 + 10 = _____

b 59 + 10 = _____

c 14 + 10 = _____

d 87 + 10 = _____

e 46 + 10 = _____

f 79 + 10 = _____

g 22 + 10 = _____

h 40 + 10 = _____

i 36 + 10 = _____

j 36 + 20 = _____

k 36 + 30 = _____

PLACE VALUE

2 Write your own equations that add 10.

● ___24___ + 10 = ___34___

a _____ + 10 = _____

b _____ + 10 = _____

c _____ + 10 = _____

3 Use the hundred chart on page 71 to subtract.

● 76 − 10 = ___66___   g 50 − 10 = _____

a 55 − 10 = _____   h 37 − 10 = _____

b 97 − 10 = _____   i 93 − 10 = _____

c 23 − 10 = _____   j 68 − 10 = _____

d 45 − 10 = _____   k 33 − 10 = _____

e 59 − 10 = _____   l 56 − 10 = _____

f 62 − 10 = _____   m 80 − 10 = _____

4 Write your own equations that subtract 10.

● ___22___ − 10 = ___12___

a _____ − 10 = _____

b _____ − 10 = _____

c _____ − 10 = _____

d _____ − 10 = _____

PLACE VALUE

100 More and 100 Less

You can use place-value patterns to find 100 more or 100 less than a number.

Example 1: Find 100 more by adding 100 to a number.

100 + 100 = 200

200 + 100 = 300

300 + 100 = 400

Pattern: Only the digit in the hundreds place changes. It goes up by 1.

235 + 100 = 335

678 + 100 = __778__

382 + 100 = __482__

Example 2: Find 100 less by subtracting 100 from a number.

500 − 100 = 400

400 − 100 = 300

300 − 100 = 200

Pattern: Only the digit in the hundreds place changes. It goes down by 1.

290 − 100 = 190

436 − 100 = __336__

279 − 100 = __179__

Your turn

1. Solve each problem.

● 439 + 100 = __539__

a 519 + 100 = _____

b 485 + 100 = _____

c 765 − 100 = _____

d 344 − 100 = _____

When you add or subtract 100, the tens place and the ones place both stay the same!

SELF CHECK   Mark how you feel

Got it!	Need help...	I don't get it
☐	 ☐	 ☐

Check your answers

How many did you get correct?

PLACE VALUE

Practice

1 Solve the addition problems.

● 700 + 100 = **800**   d   400 + 100 = _____

a   300 + 100 = _____   e   100 + 100 = _____

b   200 + 100 = _____   f   500 + 100 = _____

c   600 + 100 = _____   g   800 + 100 = _____

2 Solve the subtraction problems.

● 500 − 100 = **400**   d   100 − 100 = _____

a   300 − 100 = _____   e   600 − 100 = _____

b   400 − 100 = _____   f   900 − 100 = _____

c   200 − 100 = _____   g   700 − 100 = _____

3 Answer the questions.

● What is 100 less than 500?   **400**

a   What is 100 less than 300?   _____

b   What is 100 less than 200?   _____

c   What is 100 less than 400?   _____

d   What is 100 more than 800?   _____

e   What is 100 more than 700?   _____

f   What is 100 more than 600?   _____

PLACE VALUE

4 Solve the addition problems. Remember to look at the hundreds place.

● 254 + 100 = **354**

a 344 + 100 = _____

b 278 + 100 = _____

c 612 + 100 = _____

d 564 + 100 = _____

e 112 + 200 = _____

f 586 + 200 = _____

g 467 + 300 = _____

5 Solve the subtraction problems. Remember to look at the hundreds place.

● 534 − 100 = **434**

a 355 − 100 = _____

b 447 − 100 = _____

c 277 − 100 = _____

d 987 − 200 = _____

e 762 − 200 = _____

f 645 − 300 = _____

g 708 − 300 = _____

6 Answer the questions. Remember to look at the hundreds place.

● What is 100 less than 598? **498**

a What is 100 less than 430? _____

b What is 100 less than 309? _____

c What is 100 less than 461? _____

d What is 100 more than 287? _____

e What is 100 more than 888? _____

f What is 100 more than 525? _____

Place Value Review

1 Write each amount in expanded form.

a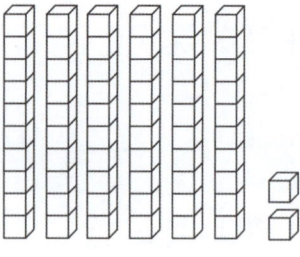

_____ tens _____ ones

_____ + _____ = _____

c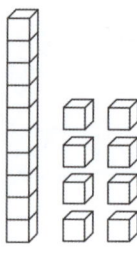

_____ ten _____ ones

_____ + _____ = _____

b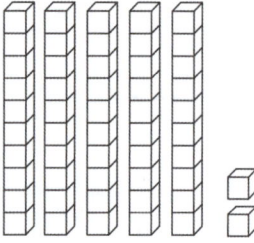

_____ tens _____ ones

_____ + _____ = _____

d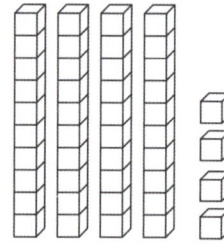

_____ tens _____ ones

_____ + _____ = _____

2 Complete each comparison. Use the words *is greater than*, *is less than*, or *is equal to*.

a 36 _____ 38

b 99 _____ 77

c 69 _____ 67

d 24 _____ 24

e 12 _____ 21

f 44 _____ 55

g 80 _____ 90

h 34 _____ 54

Review

PLACE VALUE

3 Write <, =, or > to make each comparison true.

a 43 ◯ 87   e 65 ◯ 96

b 55 ◯ 66   f 41 ◯ 14

c 28 ◯ 24   g 32 ◯ 32

d 70 ◯ 70   h 56 ◯ 67

4 Circle the numbers that fit each rule.

a greater than 40

44, 24, 49, 15

c greater than 26

22, 25, 29, 30

b equal to 29

29, 12, 92, 39

d less than 78

80, 88, 79, 74

5 Circle the larger amount in each set.

a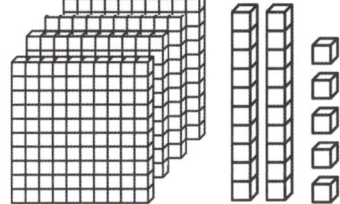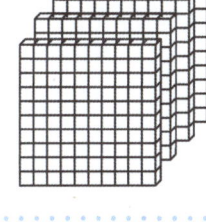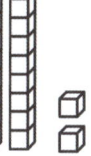

b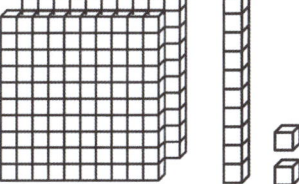

c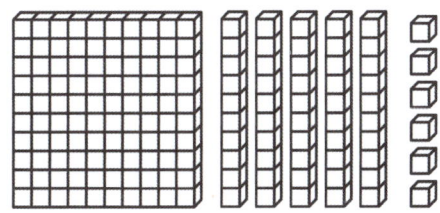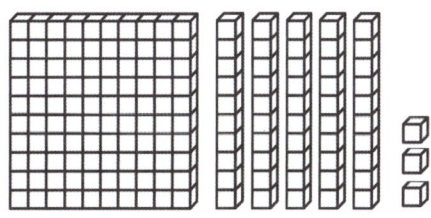

PLACE VALUE

Review

6 Use the hundred chart. Find the answers.

1	2	3	4	5	6	7	8	9	10
11	12	13	14	15	16	17	18	19	20
21	22	23	24	25	26	27	28	29	30
31	32	33	34	35	36	37	38	39	40
41	42	43	44	45	46	47	48	49	50
51	52	53	54	55	56	57	58	59	60
61	62	63	64	65	66	67	68	69	70
71	72	73	74	75	76	77	78	79	80
81	82	83	84	85	86	87	88	89	90
91	92	93	94	95	96	97	98	99	100

a 45 – 10 = _____ **d** 16 – 10 = _____ **g** 33 + 10 = _____

b 67 + 10 = _____ **e** 76 + 10 = _____ **h** 50 – 20 = _____

c 23 + 10 = _____ **f** 89 – 10 = _____ **i** 58 + 20 = _____

7 Answer the questions.

a What is 100 less than 400?   **c** What is 100 less than 563?

_____   _____

b What is 100 less than 300?   **d** What is 100 more than 765?

_____   _____

8 Solve the problems.

a 600 + 100 = _____   **c** 200 + 100 = _____   **e** 600 + 100 = _____

b 200 – 100 = _____   **d** 100 – 100 = _____   **f** 500 – 100 = _____

Add One- and Two-Digit Numbers

When you add a two-digit and a one-digit number together, start with the two-digit number. Then, add the smaller number.

Example 1: Count on from the bigger number. You can count on with your fingers.

23 + 6 = __29__

25 26 27   29
24   28

Example 2: You can use a hundred chart to count on.

41 + 6 = __47__

1	2	3	4	5	6	7	8	9	10
11	12	13	14	15	16	17	18	19	20
21	22	23	24	25	26	27	28	29	30
31	32	33	34	35	36	37	38	39	40
41	42	43	44	45	46	47	48	49	50
51	52	53	54	55	56	57	58	59	60
61	62	63	64	65	66	67	68	69	70
71	72	73	74	75	76	77	78	79	80
81	82	83	84	85	86	87	88	89	90
91	92	93	94	95	96	97	98	99	100

 **Your turn**

1 Count on to solve the problems. You can use your fingers to help you.

- 72 + 6 = __78__

a 62 + 7 = _____

b 24 + 8 = _____

c 12 + 9 = _____

> Addition problems can also be written vertically.
>
>   3 6
> +   6
> ─────

SELF CHECK   Mark how you feel

Got it!    Need help...    I don't get it

Check your answers
How many did you get correct?

ADDITION

Practice

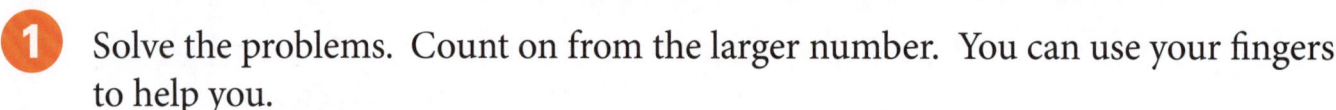

1 Solve the problems. Count on from the larger number. You can use your fingers to help you.

● 25 + 4 = __29__

a 21 + 7 = _____

b 34 + 5 = _____

c 3 + 28 = _____

d 6 + 82 = _____

e 52 + 8 = _____

f 60 + 3 = _____

g 15 + 8 = _____

h 32 + 8 = _____

i 41 + 5 = _____

2 Solve the problems. Count on from the larger number. You can use your fingers to help you.

● 46
  + 3
  ―――
   49

a   72
  + 5
  ―――

b   90
  + 8
  ―――

c   36
  + 6
  ―――

d   27
  + 5
  ―――

e   35
  + 5
  ―――

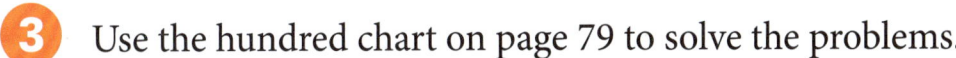

ADDITION

3 Use the hundred chart on page 79 to solve the problems.

● 44 + 9 = __53__   e 73 + 5 = _____

a 53 + 7 = _____   f 80 + 4 = _____

b 6 + 11 = _____   g 27 + 8 = _____

c 9 + 40 = _____   h 91 + 6 = _____

d 62 + 8 = _____   i 58 + 8 = _____

4 Use the hundred chart to solve the problems.

●   5 7
  +   4
   6 1

c   9 3
  +   2

a   6 3
  +   2

d   4 4
  +   4

b   7 1
  +   1

e   8 5
  +   5

ADDITION

Use Base-Ten Blocks

You can use base-ten blocks to help you solve addition problems.

Base-ten blocks show the value of each digit in a number.

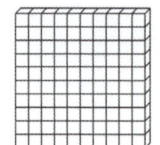 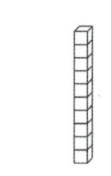

A flat shows 100s.   A rod shows 10s.   A cube shows 1s.

Example 1:

These blocks show 24.   These blocks show 15.   Together, they show 39.

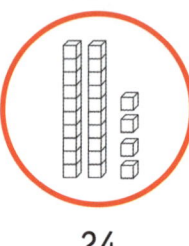 + 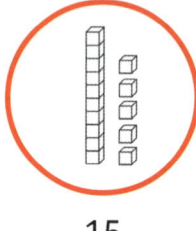 =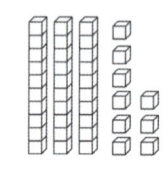

24   15   39

1 Add the numbers. Write the answers.

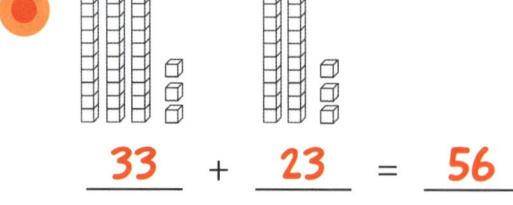

<u>33</u> + <u>23</u> = <u>56</u>

a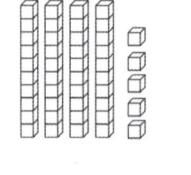

____ + ____ = ____

You can draw a ☐ for a flat, a | for a rod, and a • for a cube.

SELF CHECK Mark how you feel

Got it!  ☐   Need help...  ☐   I don't get it 😠 ☐

Check your answers
How many did you get correct?

Practice

ADDITION

1 Use the base-ten blocks to write addition equations.

●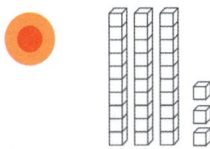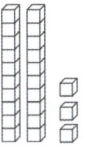

33 + 23 = **56**

b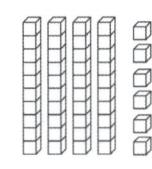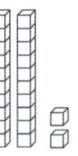

___ + ___ = ___

a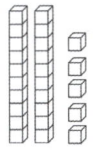

___ + ___ = ___

c

___ + ___ = ___

2 Draw base-ten blocks for each addition problem. Write the answers.

●

21 + 21 = **42**

c

40 + 15 = ___

a

24 + 15 = ___

d

32 + 20 = ___

b

31 + 47 = ___

e

23 + 12 = ___

ADDITION

3 Use the base-ten blocks to write addition equations. Remember, a flat shows 100.

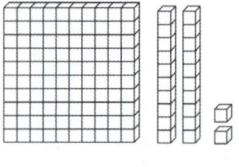 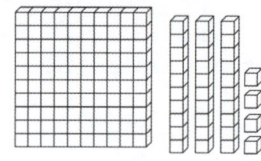

___122___ + ___134___ = ___256___

a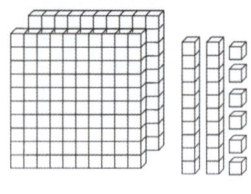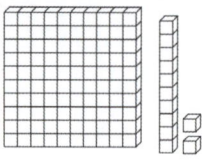

_____ + _____ = _____

b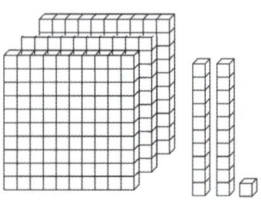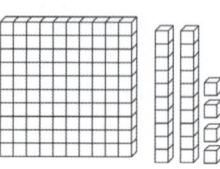

_____ + _____ = _____

4 Draw base-ten blocks to show each number. Solve the problems.

120 + 56 = ___176___

a

130 + 42 = _____

b

110 + 17 = _____

c

235 + 20 = _____

d

127 + 31 = _____

e

215 + 12 = _____

ADDITION

Addition with Number Lines

You can use a number line to solve addition problems.

Example 1: 12 + 6 = ?

Start at the larger number. Draw jumps to show how much you add. Where do you land? That is your answer.

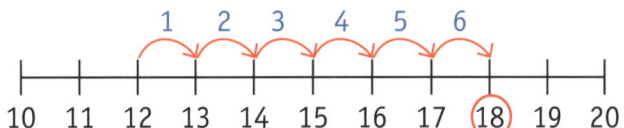

12 + 6 = **18**

Example 2: 25 + 16 = ?

To add larger numbers, you can jump by tens and ones.

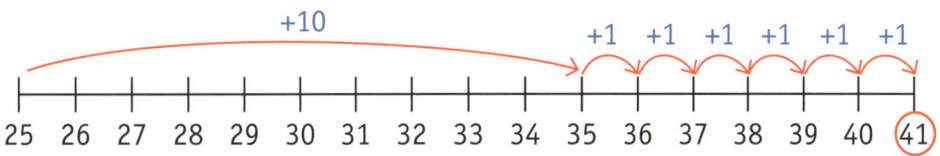

First, jump by tens. Then, jump by ones. Count forward to find out where you land. That is your answer.

25 + 16 = **41**

Your turn

① Use a number line to solve each problem. Circle the answer on the number line. Then, write the answer.

● 15 + 22 = **37**

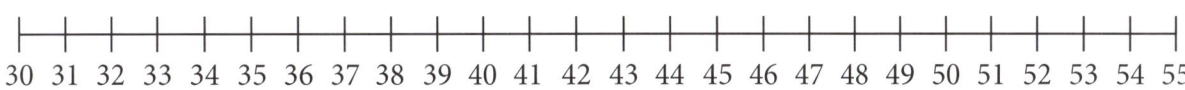

a 34 + 21 = _____

(number line from 30 to 55)

SELF CHECK Mark how you feel

Got it!   Need help...   I don't get it

Check your answers
How many did you get correct?

ADDITION

1 Use the number line to solve each problem.

● 12 + 5 = **17**

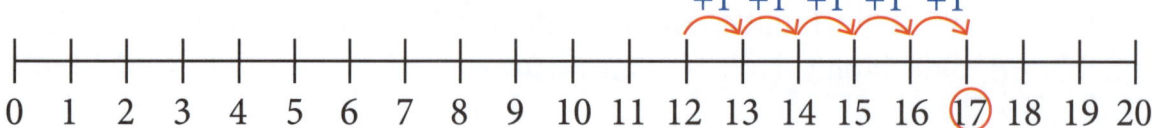

a 11 + 6 = ____

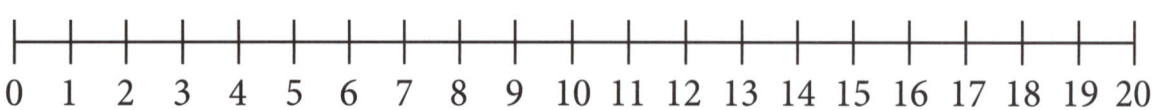

b 18 + 5 = ____

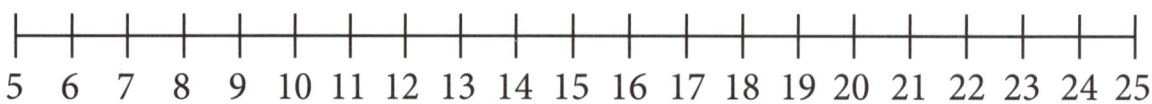

c 14 + 8 = ____

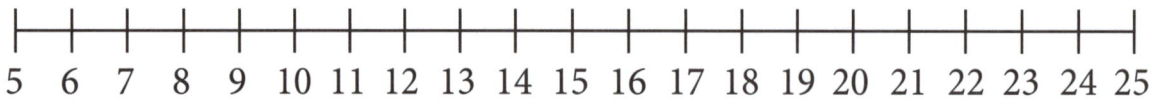

d 17 + 4 = ____

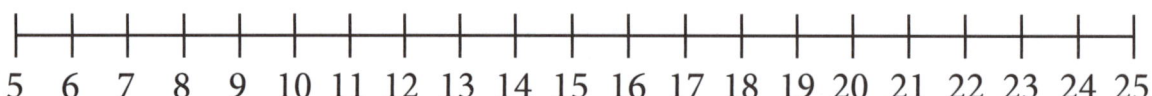

e 21 + 7 = ____

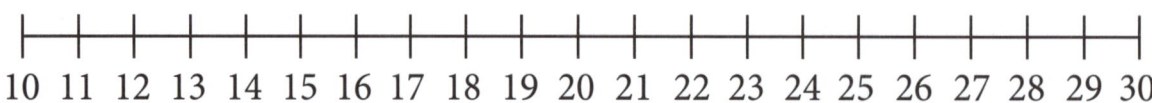

f 12 + 9 = ____

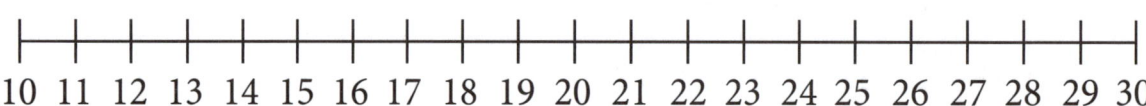

ADDITION

2 Use the number line to solve each problem. Label each jump +10 or +1 to show how much they are worth.

● 42 + 12 = __54__

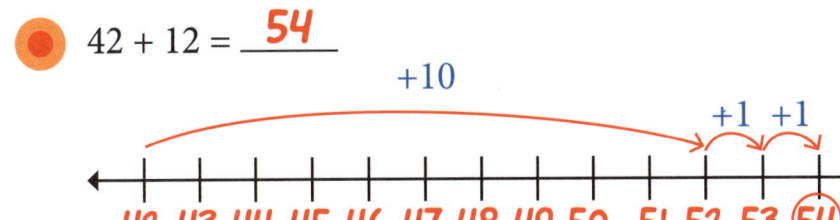

a 25 + 16 = _____

b 34 + 16 = _____

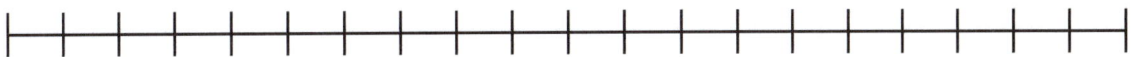

c 20 + 18 = _____

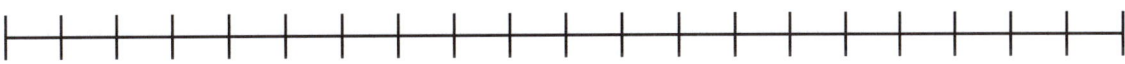

d 32 + 24 = _____

e 64 + 21 = _____

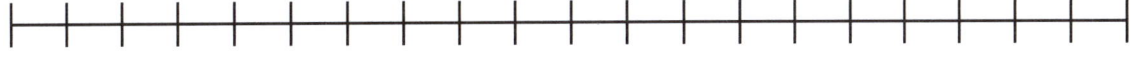

f 38 + 15 = _____

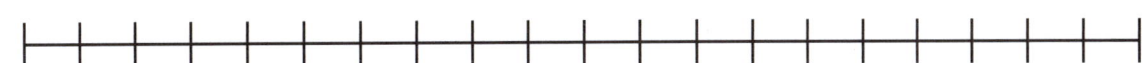

ADDITION

Add Tens and Ones

You can use what you know about place value to add tens and ones separately.

Example 1: 35 + 21 = ?

Add the tens, and then add the ones. Then, add those amounts together to get an answer.

30 + 20 = 50

5 + 1 = 6   50 + 6 = 56

Example 2: 48 + 25 = ?

40 + 20 = 60

8 + 5 = 13

60 + 13 = 73

Example 3: 57 + 15 = ?

50 + 10 = __60__

7 + 5 = __12__

__60__ + __12__ = __72__

1 Solve the tens and ones separately. Write the final equation with the answer.

● 33 + 12 = ?

30 + 10 = __40__

3 + 2 = __5__

__40__ + __5__ = __45__

a 35 + 35 = ?

30 + 30 = ____

5 + 5 = ____

____ + ____ = ____

b 22 + 36 = ?

20 + 30 = ____

2 + 6 = ____

____ + ____ = ____

SELF CHECK — Mark how you feel

Got it!   Need help...  I don't get it

Check your answers — How many did you get correct?

Practice

ADDITION

1 Solve the tens and ones separately. Write the final equation with the answer.

● 49 + 46 = ?

40 + 40 = __80__

9 + 6 = __15__

__80__ + __15__ = __95__

b 29 + 14 = ?

20 + 10 = _____

9 + 4 = _____

_____ + _____ = _____

a 69 + 32 = ?

60 + 30 = _____

9 + 2 = _____

_____ + _____ = _____

c 18 + 18 = ?

10 + 10 = _____

8 + 8 = _____

_____ + _____ = _____

2 Write the equations to solve the tens and ones separately. Then, write the final equation with the answer.

● 54 + 22 = ?

__50__ + __20__ = __70__

__4__ + __2__ = __6__

__70__ + __6__ = __76__

b 62 + 33 = ?

_____ + _____ = _____

_____ + _____ = _____

_____ + _____ = _____

a 34 + 59 = ?

_____ + _____ = _____

_____ + _____ = _____

_____ + _____ = _____

c 16 + 72 = ?

_____ + _____ = _____

_____ + _____ = _____

_____ + _____ = _____

ADDITION

Unknown Addends

An addend is a number that is added to another number. Two addends make a sum. The sum is the answer to an addition problem.

You can solve addition problems when you don't know both addends.

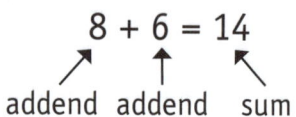

Example 1: How can you find the unknown addend: 8 + ? = 14? You can count on from 8 to get to 14.

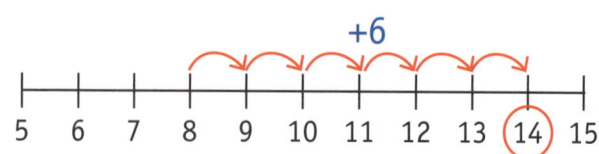

It took 6 jumps, so 8 + **6** = 14.

Example 2: You can subtract 14 − 8 to find the unknown addend. Remember how addition and subtraction are related.

14 − 8 = 6, so 8 + 6 = 14

Your turn

1 Write the unknown addend. Use a number line.

●   9 + **8** = 17

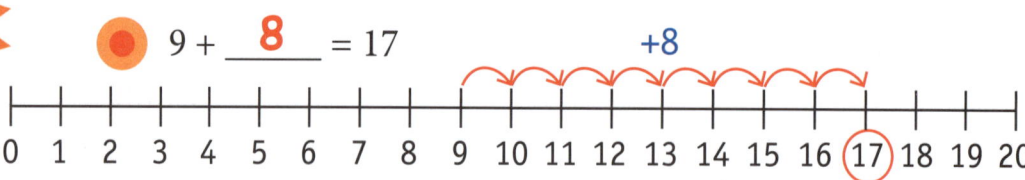

a   7 + _____ = 15

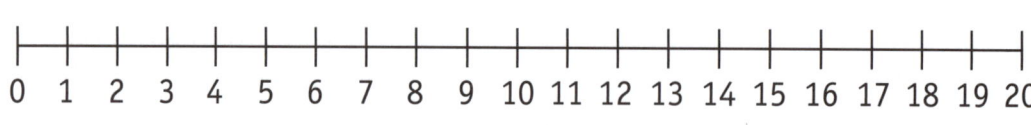

Think about fact families! Addition and subtraction equations are related.

2 Write the unknown addend. Use a related subtraction problem.

●   6 + **9** = 15   **a**   8 + _____ = 22

15 − 6 = **9**   22 − 8 = _____

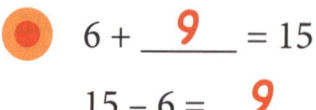

SELF CHECK   Mark how you feel

Got it!   Need help...   I don't get it

Check your answers
How many did you get correct?

Practice

ADDITION

1 Write the unknown addend. Use a number line.

● 3 + __12__ = 15

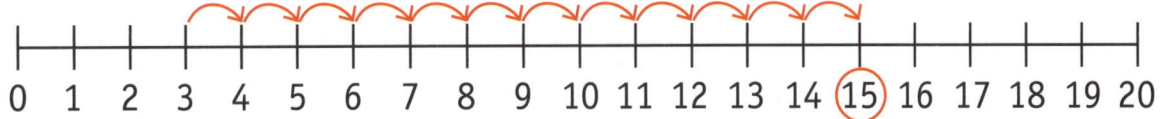

a 6 + _____ = 11

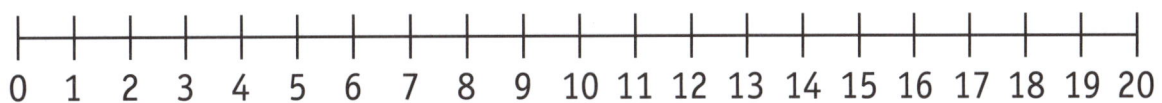

b 5 + _____ = 12

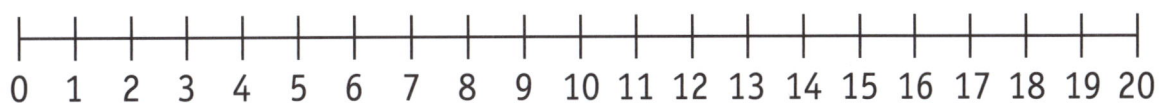

2 Write the unknown addend. Use a related subtraction problem.

● 42 + __8__ = 50   **b** 26 + _____ = 36

  50 − 42 = __8__   36 − 26 = _____

a 11 + _____ = 20   **c** 15 + _____ = 30

  20 − 11 = _____   30 − 15 = _____

3 Write the unknown addend. Use any strategy.

● 7 + __6__ = 13   **c** 3 + _____ = 10

a 8 + _____ = 12   **d** 12 + _____ = 25

b 15 + _____ = 23   **e** 10 + _____ = 28

© Shell Education   146444—Catch-Up Math   91

ADDITION

Add Three Numbers

You can solve equations and word problems where you add three numbers together.

Example 1: Practice adding three numbers. Look for two numbers that are easy to add together first. Then, add on.

```
   5  ↖ Since 5 + 5 is a double, you can
   7  ↙ add that first. Then, add the 7.
 + 5
 ----
  1 7
```

5 + 5 = 10

10 + 7 = 17

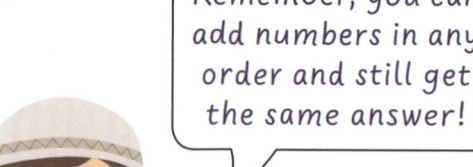

Remember, you can add numbers in any order and still get the same answer!

Example 2: There were ②dogs at the park. Then, ④more joined. Next, ⑧dogs came. How many dogs were there <u>in all</u>?

Circle the numbers in a word problem. Underline the clues. You can draw a picture to help you. Then, write and solve an equation.

```
   2  🐕🐕
   4  🐕🐕🐕🐕
 + 8  🐕🐕🐕🐕🐕🐕🐕🐕
 ----
  14
```

Your turn

1 Solve each problem.

●
```
   8
   2
 + 5
 ----
  1 5
```

b
```
   6
   6
 + 4
```

a
```
   7
   4
 + 3
```

c
```
   4
   4
 + 5
```

SELF CHECK Mark how you feel

Got it! 😊 ☐   Need help... 😐 ☐   I don't get it 😟 ☐

Check your answers How many did you get correct?

Practice

ADDITION

1 Solve each problem. You can add the numbers in any order.

```
      5                    e      6
      1                           4
   +  7                        +  5
   ─────                        ─────
     13
```

```
a     3                    f      1
      7                           6
   +  8                        +  9
   ─────                        ─────
```

```
b     9                    g      4
      9                           8
   +  2                        +  6
   ─────                        ─────
```

```
c     5                    h      3
      6                           3
   +  5                        +  3
   ─────                        ─────
```

```
d     2                    i      1
      2                           6
   +  7                        +  3
   ─────                        ─────
```

ADDITION

2 Read each word problem. Write and solve an equation. Draw a picture, if it helps you.

● A store sold popular video games. They sold 8 of one game. Then, they sold 4 of another and 6 of a third game. How many video games did they sell in all?

```
    8
    4
+   6
   18
```

a Matteo has 6 basketballs. He also has 4 soccer balls and 3 baseballs. How many balls does he have in all?

b Jesse collects coins. He got 8 coins from his mom. He got 6 coins from his dad. He got 2 coins from his uncle. How many coins does he have in all?

c Mia baked cupcakes. She made 4 with vanilla frosting. She made 6 with chocolate frosting. She made 3 with strawberry frosting. How many cupcakes did she make in all?

d Jin read books all week. On Monday, he read 4 books. On Tuesday, he read 3 books. On Wednesday, he read 4 books. How many books did he read in all?

e Mr. Harrison had art materials. He had 4 crayons. He also had 6 colored pencils and 7 chalk pastels. How many materials did Mr. Harrison have in all?

ADDITION

Addition with Regrouping

You may need to regroup when you add numbers together. Sometimes, the ones add up to 10 or more. This means you have to make groups of 10.

Example 1:
You can regroup by drawing base-ten blocks. Group a 10 by circling 10 ones. Move them to the tens place.

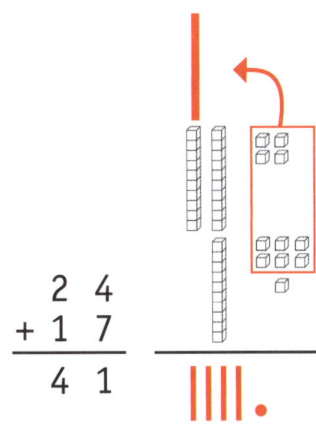

```
   2 4
 + 1 7
 ─────
   4 1
```

Example 2:

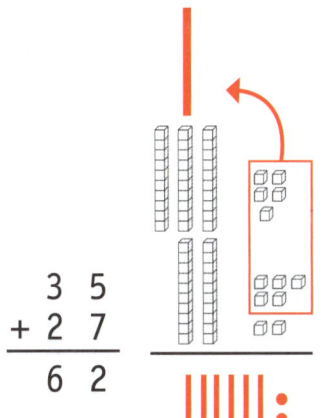

```
   3 5
 + 2 7
 ─────
   6 2
```

SCAN to watch video

Your turn

1. Show how to regroup by circling the group of 10. Write the answer.

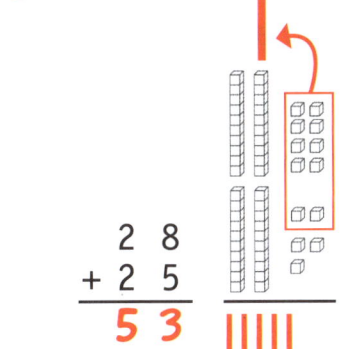

```
   2 8
 + 2 5
 ─────
   5 3
```

a

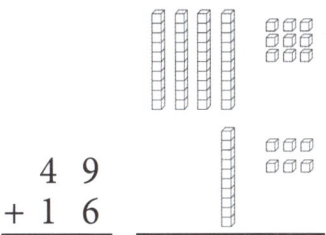

```
   4 9
 + 1 6
 ─────
```

SELF CHECK — Mark how you feel: Got it! | Need help... | I don't get it

Check your answers — How many did you get correct?

ADDITION

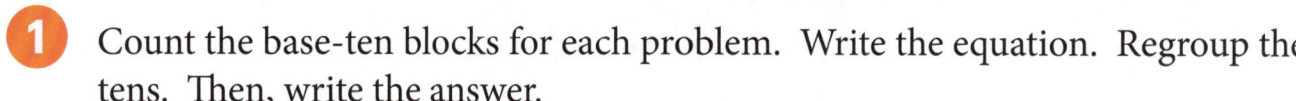

1. Count the base-ten blocks for each problem. Write the equation. Regroup the tens. Then, write the answer.

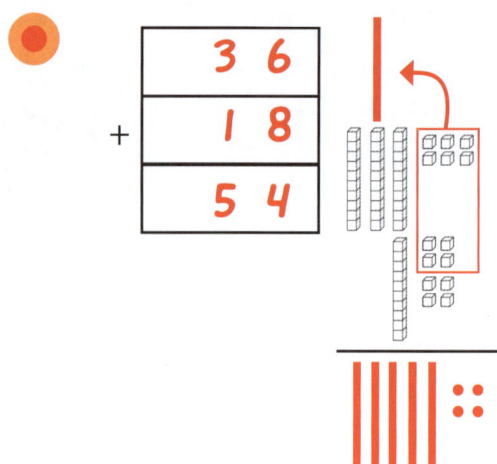

a.

b.

c.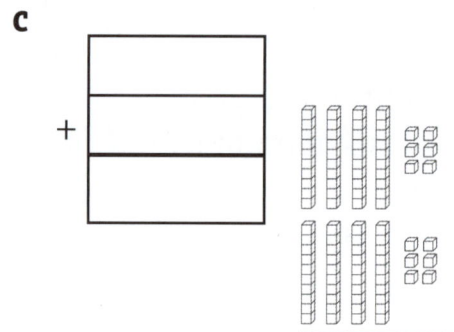

d.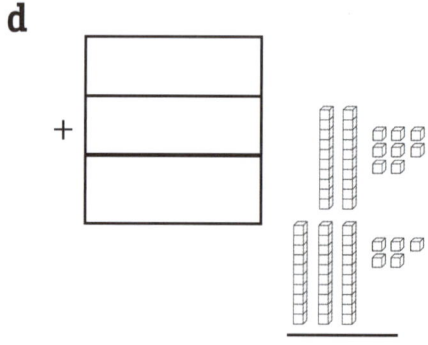

e.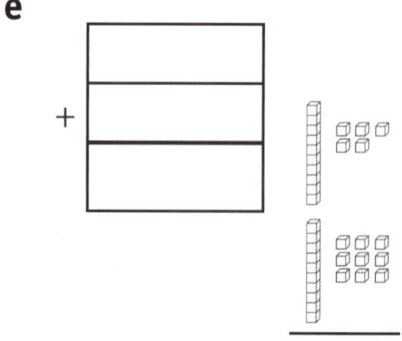

ADDITION

2 Draw the base-ten blocks for each problem. Regroup the tens. Then, write the answer.

●
```
   5 5
+  2 6
───────
   8 1
```

c
```
   2 9
+  1 9
───────
```

a
```
   2 4
+  2 8
───────
```

d
```
   2 5
+  1 5
───────
```

b
```
   3 6
+  1 5
───────
```

e
```
   3 8
+  2 6
───────
```

ADDITION

Standard Addition Algorithm

An algorithm is a strategy that follows the same steps each time you use it.

Use the standard algorithm to solve addition problems.

Step 1: Add the ones place. Regroup. Add the extra 10 to the tens place.

Step 2: Add the tens place. Make sure to add any regrouped tens.

SCAN to watch video

```
  Tens Ones
    1
    5 6
+   2 5
  -------
    8 1
```

Your turn

1 Practice the algorithm. Solve the problems.

```
    1
    2 6
+   1 5
  -------
    4 1
```

a
```
    3 4
+   1 8
  -------
```

b
```
    5 3
+   2 9
  -------
```

You must start in the ones place when you use an addition algorithm.

SELF CHECK — Mark how you feel
Got it! Need help... I don't get it

Check your answers
How many did you get correct?

98 146444—Catch-Up Math   © Shell Education

ADDITION

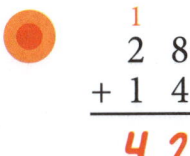 Solve the problems. Use the standard algorithm. Show how you regroup.

```
    1
    2 8
  + 1 4
  -------
    4 2
```

e
```
    6 5
  + 2 7
  -------
```

a
```
    1 7
  + 1 7
  -------
```

f
```
    1 9
  + 1 7
  -------
```

b
```
    5 4
  + 2 8
  -------
```

g
```
    6 7
  + 1 4
  -------
```

c
```
    3 7
  + 2 5
  -------
```

h
```
    2 9
  + 1 3
  -------
```

d
```
    2 8
  + 2 6
  -------
```

i
```
    4 5
  + 2 7
  -------
```

ADDITION

2 Solve the problems. Only regroup when it is needed.

a. 25
   +13
   ___

b. 54
   +22
   ___

c. 47
   +14
   ___

d. 53
   +13
   ___

e. 57
   +34
   ___

f. 76
   +20
   ___

g. 48
   +25
   ___

h. 84
   +15
   ___

i. 47
   +26
   ___

j. 54
   +21
   ___

ADDITION

Add Three-Digit Numbers

You can add three-digit numbers using the same strategies used for two-digit numbers.

Example 1: You can add hundreds, tens, and ones separately.

134 + 128

Hundreds: 100 + 100 = 200

Tens: 30 + 20 = 50

Ones: 4 + 8 = 12

Total: 200 + 50 + 12 = **262**

Example 2: You can regroup with base-ten blocks. Group 10 ones by circling.

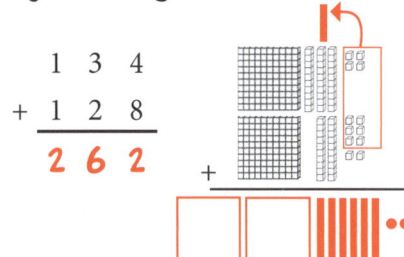

```
  1 3 4
+ 1 2 8
───────
  2 6 2
```

Example 3: You can use the standard algorithm with three-digit numbers.

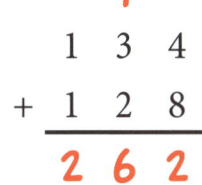

```
    1
  1 3 4
+ 1 2 8
───────
  2 6 2
```

Your turn

1 Add hundreds, tens, and ones separately. Then, add the sums.

● 126 + 147 = ?

Hundreds: __100__ + __100__ = __200__

Tens: __20__ + __40__ = __60__

Ones: __6__ + __7__ = __13__

Total: __200__ + __60__ + __13__ = __273__

> Make sure to line up the numbers by place value.

a   156 + 148 = ?

Hundreds: _____ + _____ = _____

Tens: _____ + _____ = _____

Ones: _____ + _____ = _____

Total: _____ + _____ + _____ = _____

SELF CHECK   Mark how you feel

Got it! ☺ ☐   Need help... 😐 ☐   I don't get it 😟 ☐

Check your answers
How many did you get correct?

ADDITION  **Practice**

1 Draw base-ten blocks. Regroup the ones into tens if you need to. Write the answers.

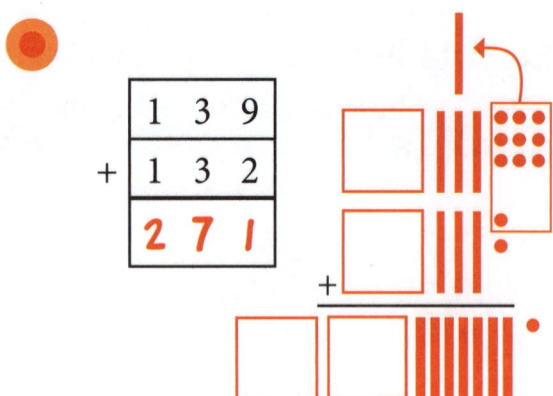

```
  1 3 9
+ 1 3 2
  2 7 1
```

c
```
  2 7 3
+ 1 1 8
```

a
```
  1 5 6
+ 1 1 7
```

d
```
  3 0 6
+ 2 2 9
```

b
```
  2 3 6
+ 1 5 7
```

e
```
  2 3 7
+ 1 5 5
```

102 146444—Catch-Up Math © Shell Education

ADDITION

2 Add the hundreds, tens, and ones separately. Then, add the sums.

 157 + 128

Hundreds: 100 + 100 = **200**

Tens: 50 + 20 = **70**

Ones: 7 + 8 = **15**

Total: **200** + **70** + **15** = **285**

b 315 + 166

Hundreds: ____ + ____ = ____

Tens: ____ + ____ = ____

Ones: ____ + ____ = ____

Total: ____ + ____ + ____ = ____

a 214 + 228

Hundreds: ____ + ____ = ____

Tens: ____ + ____ = ____

Ones: ____ + ____ = ____

Total: ____ + ____ + ____ = ____

c 218 + 145

Hundreds: ____ + ____ = ____

Tens: ____ + ____ = ____

Ones: ____ + ____ = ____

Total: ____ + ____ + ____ = ____

3 Use the standard algorithm. Solve the problems.

```
    1
  2 1 8
+ 1 5 5
-------
  3 7 3
```

c
```
  2 3 6
+ 1 4 4
-------
```

a
```
  1 5 5
+ 1 2 8
-------
```

d
```
  1 4 9
+ 1 4 5
-------
```

b
```
  2 4 9
+ 1 1 3
-------
```

e
```
  2 0 6
+ 1 3 5
-------
```

Addition Review

1 Count on to solve each problem.

a $26 + 5 = \underline{}$

b $42 + 6 = \underline{}$

c $4 + 31 = \underline{}$

d $7 + 81 = \underline{}$

e $50 + 8 = \underline{}$

f $62 + 5 = \underline{}$

g $41 + 4 = \underline{}$

h $\begin{array}{r} 22 \\ +5 \\ \hline \end{array}$

i $\begin{array}{r} 61 \\ +6 \\ \hline \end{array}$

j $\begin{array}{r} 73 \\ +5 \\ \hline \end{array}$

k $\begin{array}{r} 60 \\ +8 \\ \hline \end{array}$

l $\begin{array}{r} 42 \\ +6 \\ \hline \end{array}$

m $\begin{array}{r} 22 \\ +5 \\ \hline \end{array}$

n $\begin{array}{r} 33 \\ +6 \\ \hline \end{array}$

Review

ADDITION

2 Count the base-ten blocks. Write and solve the equations.

a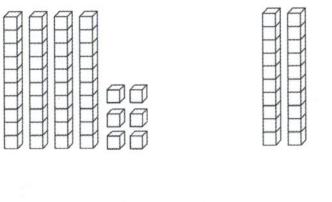

___ + ___ = ___

f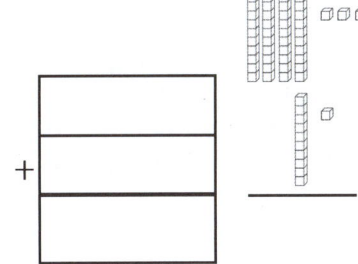

b

___ + ___ = ___

g

c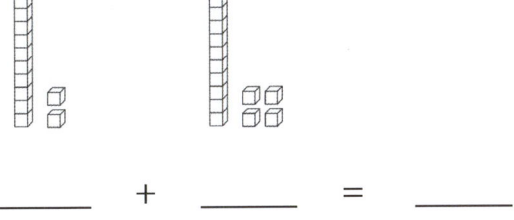

___ + ___ = ___

h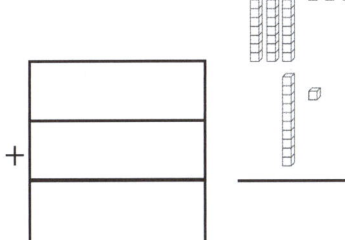

d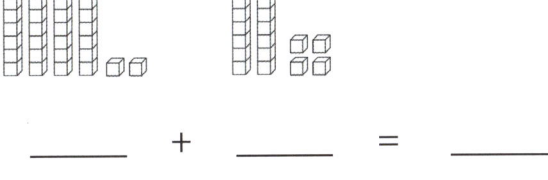

___ + ___ = ___

i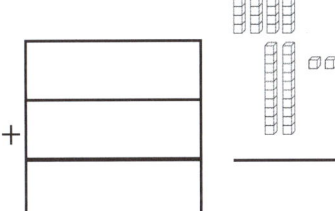

e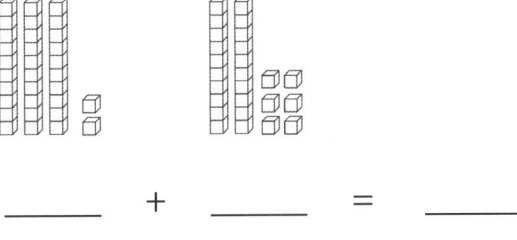

___ + ___ = ___

j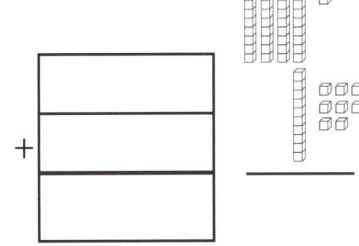

ADDITION

Review

3 Use the number lines to solve the problems. Show your jumps.

a 11 + 7 = _____

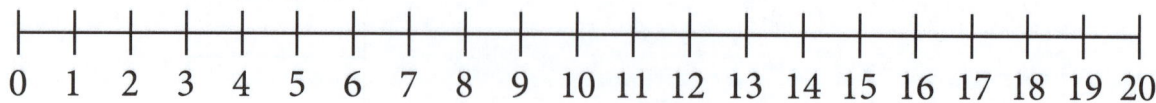

b 12 + 4 = _____

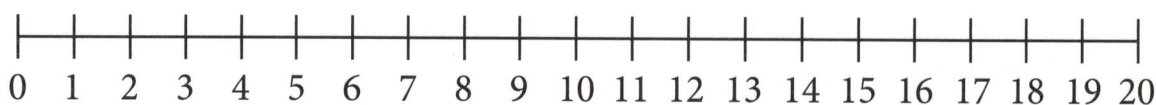

c 19 + 3 = _____

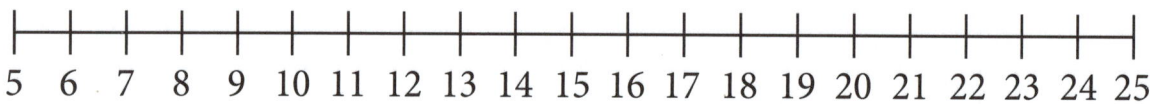

d 20 + 3 = _____

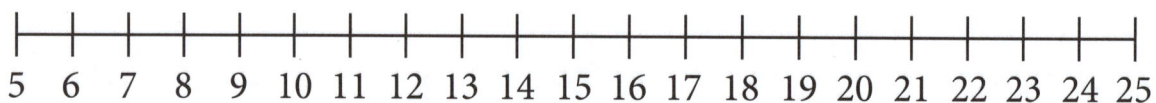

e 15 + 7 = _____

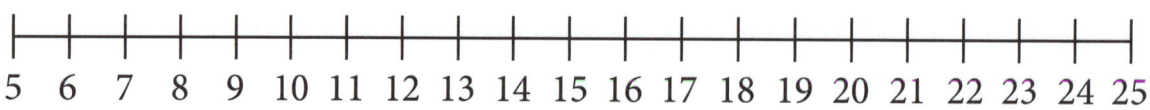

f 35 + 18 = _____

g 53 + 12 = _____

Review

ADDITION

4 Add the tens and ones separately. Write the final equation with the answer.

a   48 + 39

40 + 30 = _____

8 + 9 = _____

_____ + _____ = _____

c   37 + 25

30 + 20 = _____

7 + 5 = _____

_____ + _____ = _____

b   67 + 22

60 + 20 = _____

7 + 2 = _____

_____ + _____ = _____

d   16 + 16

10 + 10 = _____

6 + 6 = _____

_____ + _____ = _____

5 Add the tens and ones separately. Write the final equation with the answer.

a   52 + 24

_____ + _____ = _____

_____ + _____ = _____

_____ + _____ = _____

c   72 + 15

_____ + _____ = _____

_____ + _____ = _____

_____ + _____ = _____

b   15 + 37

_____ + _____ = _____

_____ + _____ = _____

_____ + _____ = _____

d   28 + 28

_____ + _____ = _____

_____ + _____ = _____

_____ + _____ = _____

ADDITION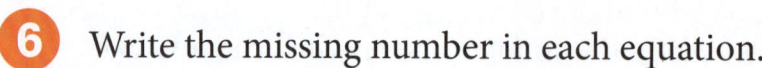

Review

6 Write the missing number in each equation.

a
12 + ____ = 19

19 − 12 = ____

b
30 + ____ = 40

40 − 30 = ____

c
15 + ____ = 27

27 − 15 = ____

d
8 + ____ = 22

22 − 8 = ____

7 Solve each problem.

a
```
   4
   7
 + 6
```

b
```
   3
   2
 + 5
```

c
```
   1
   4
 + 8
```

d
```
   2
   7
 + 3
```

e
```
   5
   6
 + 8
```

f
```
   5
   2
 + 4
```

Review

ADDITION

8 Read each word problem. Write and solve an equation. Draw a picture if it helps you.

a. There were 2 birds in the puddle. Then, 3 more joined. Next, 3 birds landed there. How many birds were there in all?

b. Lily has 5 red stickers. She has 3 green stickers. She also has 6 blue stickers. How many stickers does she have in all?

c. Destiny was counting the stars. First, she counted 8 stars. Then, she counted 6 more. Finally, she counted 5 more. How many stars did she count in all?

9 Solve each problem. Use the standard algorithm.

a.
  1 6
 + 1 5

b.
  3 2
 + 2 1

c.
  8 1
 + 1 4

d.
  3 7
 + 2 5

e.
  6 6
 + 2 4

f.
  1 8
 + 1 5

SUBTRACTION

Subtract One-Digit Numbers from Two-Digit Numbers

You can subtract a one-digit number from a two-digit number.

Example 1: Count back from the bigger number. You can use your hands.

28 − 5 = __23__

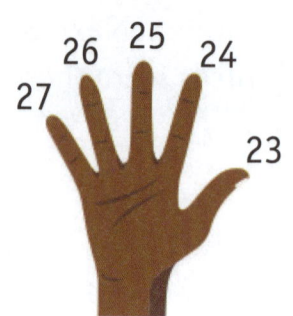

Example 2: Count back on a hundred chart.

1	2	3	4	5	6	7	8	9	10
11	12	13	14	15	16	17	18	19	20
21	22	23	24	25	26	27	28	29	30
31	32	33	34	35	36	37	38	39	40
41	42	43	44	45	46	47	48	49	50
51	52	53	54	55	56	57	58	59	60
61	62	63	64	65	66	67	68	69	70
71	72	73	74	75	76	77	78	79	80
81	82	83	84	85	86	87	88	89	90
91	92	93	94	95	96	97	98	99	100

23 − 4 = **19**

You passed over the 20 going back, so the tens place changed to 1.

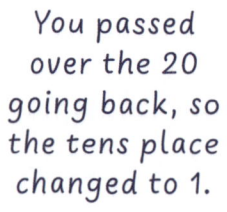

Your turn

1 Count back to subtract.

● 38 − 6 = __32__

a 28 − 3 = _____

b 16 − 5 = _____

c 29 − 8 = _____

d 36 − 3 = _____

SELF CHECK Mark how you feel

Got it! □ Need help... □ I don't get it □

Check your answers — How many did you get correct?

Practice

SUBTRACTION

1 Count back to subtract.

● 36 − 5 = __31__

a 25 − 8 = _____

b 35 − 5 = _____

c 63 − 5 = _____

d 26 − 4 = _____

e 74 − 8 = _____

f 58 − 6 = _____

g 29 − 7 = _____

h 44 − 6 = _____

i 7 7
   − 5
   ____

j 5 6
   − 4
   ____

k 7 8
   − 5
   ____

l 4 8
   − 6
   ____

m 3 5
   − 2
   ____

n 4 3
   − 4
   ____

SUBTRACTION

2 Use a hundred chart to count back.

1	2	3	4	5	6	7	8	9	10
11	12	13	14	15	16	17	18	19	20
21	22	23	24	25	26	27	28	29	30
31	32	33	34	35	36	37	38	39	40
41	42	43	44	45	46	47	48	49	50
51	52	53	54	55	56	57	58	59	60
61	62	63	64	65	66	67	68	69	70
71	72	73	74	75	76	77	78	79	80
81	82	83	84	85	86	87	88	89	90
91	92	93	94	95	96	97	98	99	100

● 64 − 8 = __56__

a 53 − 7 = _____

b 45 − 9 = _____

c 33 − 6 = _____

d 56 − 8 = _____

e 22 − 5 = _____

f 38 − 7 = _____

g   6 3
     −   4

h   5 4
     −   7

i   7 1
     −   6

j   6 5
     −   6

Subtraction with Base-Ten Blocks

You can use base-ten blocks to help you solve subtraction problems.

Base-ten blocks show the value of each digit in a number.

A flat shows 100s.   A rod shows 10s.   A cube shows 1s.

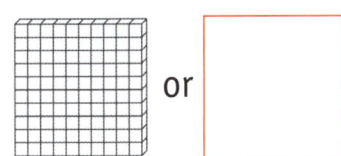   

Example 1: 36 − 5 = ?

These blocks show 36.   Cross out 5 ones.

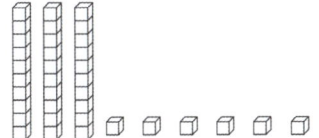   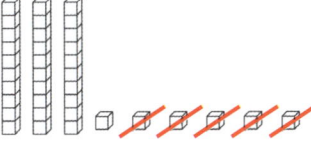   36 − 5 = __31__

Example 2: 48 − 23 = ?

These blocks show 48.   23 blocks are crossed out. 25 are left.

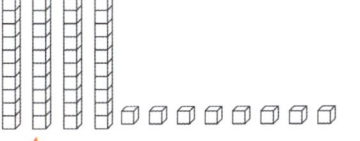      48 − 23 = __25__

Your turn

1 Use the base-ten blocks to subtract. Write the answers.

 47 − 32 = ?   47 − 32 = __15__

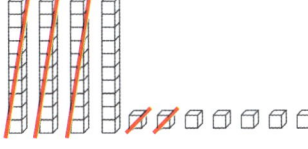

You can draw flats, rods, and cubes to solve subtraction problems.

a 28 − 16 = ?   28 − 16 = _____

SELF CHECK   Mark how you feel

Got it!   Need help...   I don't get it

Check your answers
How many did you get correct?

SUBTRACTION

Practice

1 Count each set of base-ten blocks. Write the equation that is shown.

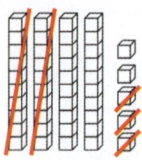

____45____ − ____23____ = ____22____

c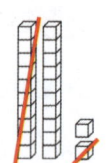

____ − ____ = ____

a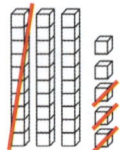

____ − ____ = ____

d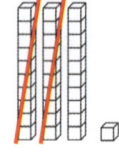

____ − ____ = ____

b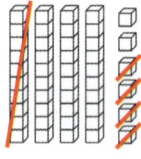

____ − ____ = ____

e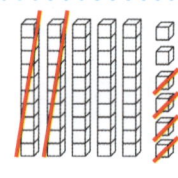

____ − ____ = ____

2 Draw base-ten blocks to show the larger number in each equation. Cross out the amount of the smaller number. Then, write your answer.

36 − 12 = ____24____

c

47 − 15 = ____

a

24 − 11 = ____

d

32 − 20 = ____

b

37 − 26 = ____

e

43 − 12 = ____

SUBTRACTION

3 Count each set of base-ten blocks. Write the equation that is shown. Remember, a flat shows 100.

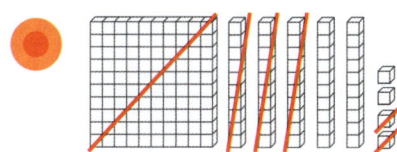
154 − 132 = __22__

c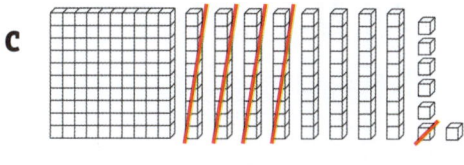
____ − ____ = ____

a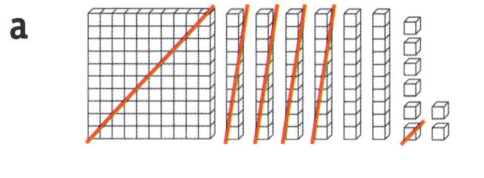
____ − ____ = ____

d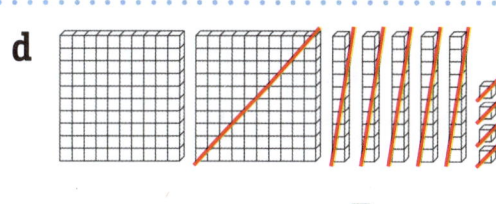
____ − ____ = ____

b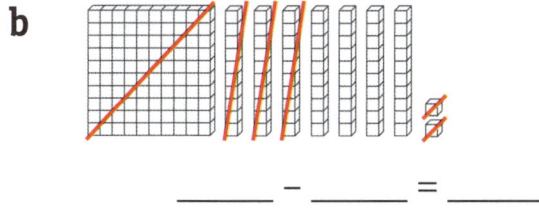
____ − ____ = ____

e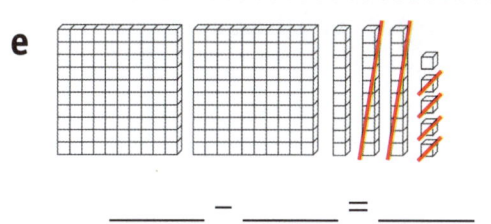
____ − ____ = ____

4 Draw base-ten blocks to show the larger number in each equation. Cross out the amount of the smaller number. Then, write your answer.

156 − 31 = __125__

c

184 − 143 = ____

a

157 − 41 = ____

d

127 − 21 = ____

b

138 − 17 = ____

e

244 − 113 = ____

SUBTRACTION

Subtraction with Number Lines

A number line can be used for subtraction problems.

Example 1: Count back on the number line.

12 − 5 = ?

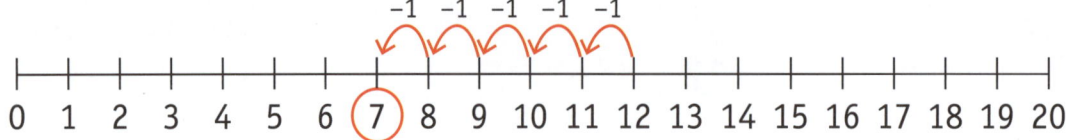

Start at the first number. Make jumps back to show how much you subtract. Where do you land? That is your answer.

12 − 5 = __7__

Example 2: You can sketch your own number line to subtract larger numbers.

25 − 12 = ?

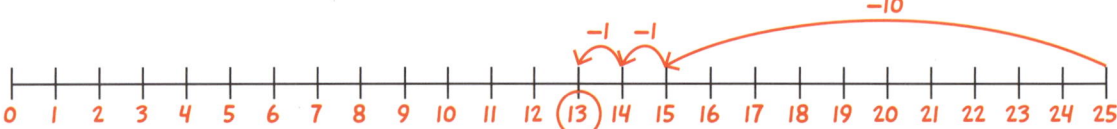

Write the larger number on the line. First, jump back by tens. Then, jump back by ones. Where do you land? That is your answer.

25 − 12 = __13__

1 Use the number line to solve each problem. Show your jumps. Write the answer.

●   15 − 8 = __7__

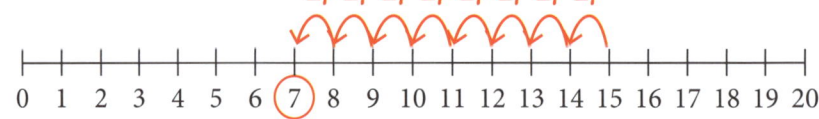

a   14 − 6 = _____

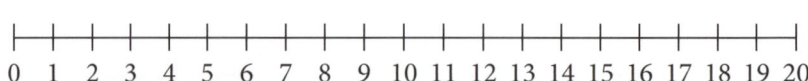

SELF CHECK   Mark how you feel

Got it!	Need help...	I don't get it
😊 ☐	😐 ☐	😟 ☐

Check your answers
How many did you get correct?

Practice

SUBTRACTION

1 Use the number line to solve each problem. Show your jumps. Write the answer.

● 13 − 5 = __8__

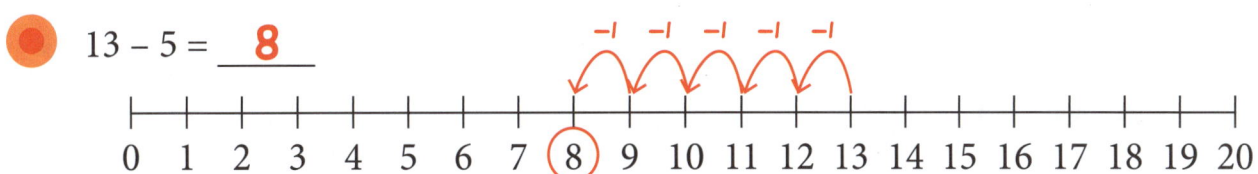

a 12 − 4 = _____

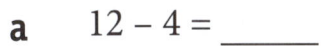

b 11 − 7 = _____

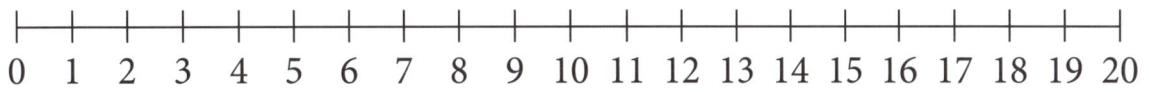

c 18 − 6 = _____

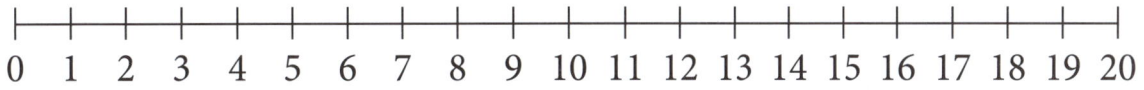

d 14 − 9 = _____

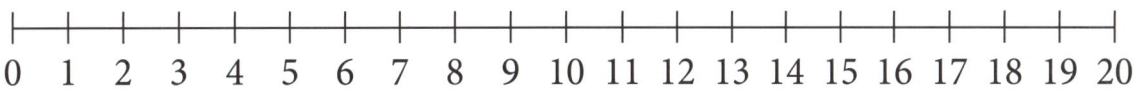

e 17 − 4 = _____

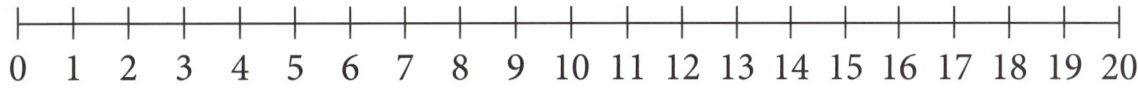

f 20 − 7 = _____

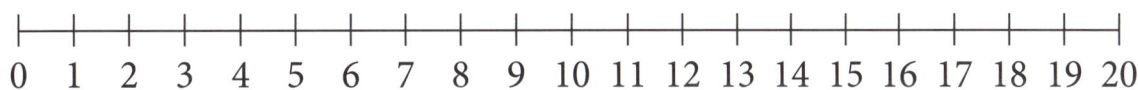

g 18 − 8 = _____

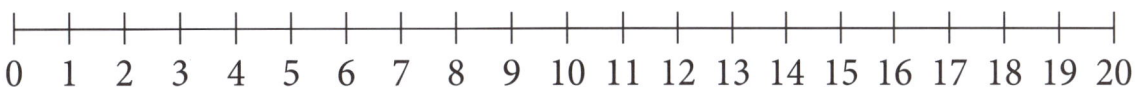

SUBTRACTION

2 Use the blank number line to solve each problem. Show your jumps. Write the answer.

● 34 − 12 = **22**

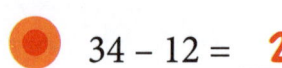

a 24 − 11 = _____

b 37 − 12 = _____

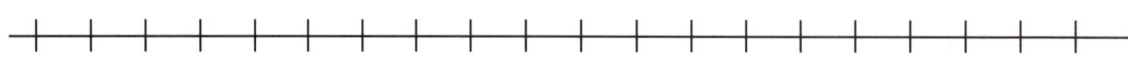

c 23 − 11 = _____

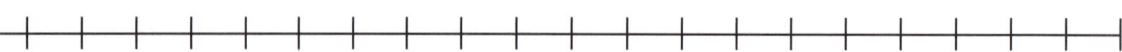

d 35 − 24 = _____

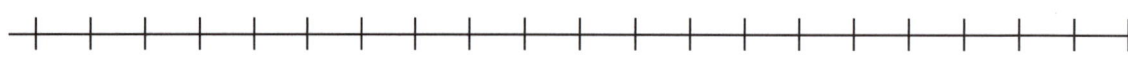

e 44 − 21 = _____

f 39 − 16 = _____

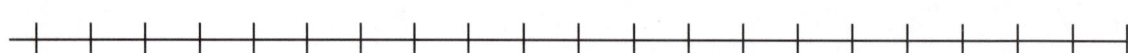

SUBTRACTION

Subtract Tens and Ones

Use what you know about place value to subtract tens and ones separately. Then, combine what is left to find your answer.

Example 1: 35 − 22 = ?

Tens: 30 − 20 = 10

Ones: 5 − 2 = 3

Total: 10 + 3 = 13

35 − 22 = 13

Example 2: 48 − 25 = ?

Tens: 40 − 20 = 20

Ones: 8 − 5 = 3

Total: 20 + 3 = 23

48 − 25 = 23

Example 3: 68 − 14 = ?

Tens: 60 − 10 = 50

Ones: 8 − 4 = 4

Total: 50 + 4 = 54

68 − 14 = 54

This strategy works when the larger number has more ones than the smaller number.

Your turn

 1 Write the missing numbers to complete each equation.

● 39 − 12 = ?

Tens: 30 − 10 = __20__

Ones: 9 − 2 = __7__

Total: __20__ + __7__ = __27__

39 − 12 = __27__

a 75 − 41 = ?

Tens: 70 − 40 = ____

Ones: 5 − 1 = ____

Total: ____ + ____ = ____

75 − 41 = ____

SELF CHECK Mark how you feel

Got it!   Need help...   I don't get it

Check your answers

How many did you get correct?

SUBTRACTION Practice

1 Write the missing numbers to complete each equation.

● 58 − 15 = ?
Tens: 50 − 10 = __40__
Ones: 8 − 5 = __3__
Total: __40__ + __3__ = __43__
58 − 15 = __43__

b 54 − 32 = ?
Tens: 50 − 30 = _____
Ones: 4 − 2 = _____
Total: _____ + _____ = _____
54 − 32 = _____

a 46 − 23 = ?
Tens: 40 − 20 = _____
Ones: 6 − 3 = _____
Total: _____ + _____ = _____
46 − 23 = _____

c 29 − 15 = ?
Tens: 20 − 10 = _____
Ones: 9 − 5 = _____
Total: _____ + _____ = _____
29 − 15 = _____

2 Subtract the tens and ones separately. Then, add together what is left. Write the final answer.

● 86 − 62 = ?
Tens: __80__ − __60__ = __20__
Ones: __6__ − __2__ = __4__
Total: __20__ + __4__ = __24__
86 − 62 = __24__

b 74 − 33 = ?
Tens: _____ − _____ = _____
Ones: _____ − _____ = _____
Total: _____ + _____ = _____
74 − 33 = _____

a 93 − 23 = ?
Tens: _____ − _____ = _____
Ones: _____ − _____ = _____
Total: _____ + _____ = _____
93 − 23 = _____

c 29 − 20 = ?
Tens: _____ − _____ = _____
Ones: _____ − _____ = _____
Total: _____ + _____ = _____
29 − 20 = _____

Add to Subtract

Subtraction can be thought of as an unknown-addend problem.

Example 1: 12 − 5 = ?

You can use a fact family to find the missing number.

A related unknown-addend problem is 5 + ? = 12.

5 + 7 = 12, so 12 − 5 = **7**

The missing number is 7.

Example 2: 10 − 4 = ?

You can use a fact family to find this missing number, too.

4 + 6 = 10, so 10 − 4 = **6**

The missing number is 6.

Fact families show how addition and subtraction are related.

1 Solve the related unknown-addend problems. Then, write the answer to the subtraction problems.

⬤   15 − 8 = ?

8 + __**7**__ = 15

15 − 8 = __**7**__

b   14 − 7 = ?

7 + _____ = 14

14 − 7 = _____

a   13 − 5 = ?

5 + _____ = 13

13 − 5 = _____

c   17 − 8 = ?

8 + _____ = 17

17 − 8 = _____

SELF CHECK   Mark how you feel

Got it! 

Need help... 

I don't get it 

Check your answers
How many did you get correct?

SUBTRACTION Practice

1 Write the missing number in each equation.

● 4 + 6 = 10, so 10 − 6 = __4__

a 4 + 4 = 8, so 8 − 4 = _____

b 5 + 9 = 14, so 14 − 9 = _____

c 11 + 5 = 16, so 16 − 11 = _____

d 3 + 5 = 8, so 8 − 3 = _____

e 10 + 7 = 17, so 17 − 7 = _____

2 Solve each related unknown-addend problem. Then, write the answer to the subtraction problem.

● 13 − 6 = ?
  6 + __7__ = 13
  13 − 6 = __7__

a 15 − 5 = ?
  5 + _____ = 15
  15 − 5 = _____

b 18 − 4 = ?
  4 + _____ = 18
  18 − 4 = _____

c 17 − 9 = ?
  9 + _____ = 17
  17 − 9 = _____

d 20 − 11 = ?
  11 + _____ = 20
  20 − 11 = _____

e 11 − 3 = ?
  3 + _____ = 11
  11 − 3 = _____

f 14 − 5 = ?
  5 + _____ = 14
  14 − 5 = _____

g 12 − 6 = ?
  6 + _____ = 12
  12 − 6 = _____

Subtraction with Regrouping

Sometimes, you need to regroup when you subtract. When this happens, use values from the tens place to have enough in the ones place to subtract.

SCAN to watch video

Regroup when you draw base-ten blocks.

- **Step 1:** You can't take 6 ones away from 3 ones. So, you have to change 1 ten into 10 ones.

$$\begin{array}{r} 4\,3 \\ -\,2\,6 \\ \hline \end{array}$$

- **Step 2:** Break up a 10 into 10 ones. You still have the same number. 4 tens and 3 ones has the same value as 3 tens and 13 ones.

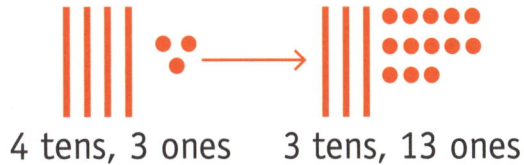
4 tens, 3 ones → 3 tens, 13 ones

- **Step 3:** Subtract the 6 ones by crossing them out. Then, cross out the 2 tens.

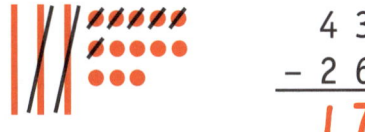

$$\begin{array}{r} 4\,3 \\ -\,2\,6 \\ \hline 1\,7 \end{array}$$

- **Step 4:** Count what is left. There are 1 ten and 7 ones. The answer is 17.

Your turn

1. Count the base-ten blocks. Regroup the tens. Cross off the amount you need to subtract. Then, write the answer.

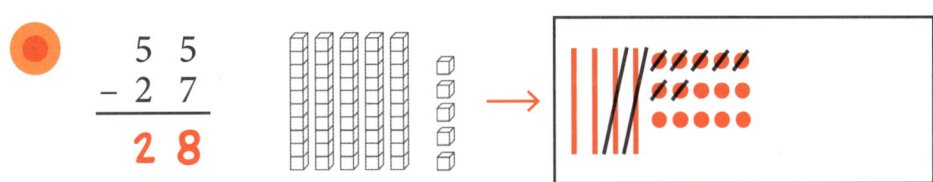

$$\begin{array}{r} 5\,5 \\ -\,2\,7 \\ \hline 2\,8 \end{array}$$

a. $\begin{array}{r} 4\,1 \\ -\,1\,6 \\ \hline \end{array}$

SELF CHECK Mark how you feel
Got it! □   Need help... □   I don't get it □

Check your answers How many did you get correct?

SUBTRACTION

Practice

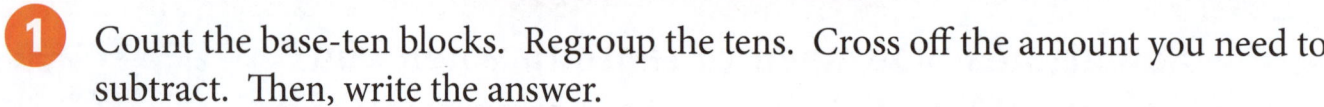

1 Count the base-ten blocks. Regroup the tens. Cross off the amount you need to subtract. Then, write the answer.

```
  5 3
- 1 8
-----
  3 5
```
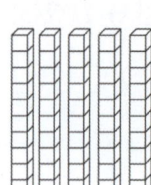 →

a
```
  6 3
- 1 5
```
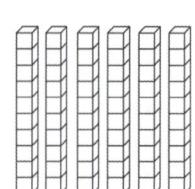 →

b
```
  4 2
- 2 7
```
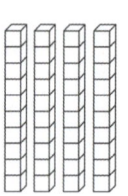 →

c
```
  7 3
- 3 6
```
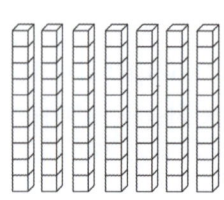 →

d
```
  6 6
- 4 9
```
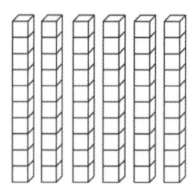 →

e
```
  3 7
- 1 8
```
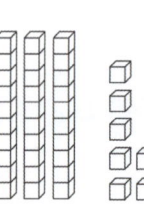 →

124   146444—Catch-Up Math   © Shell Education

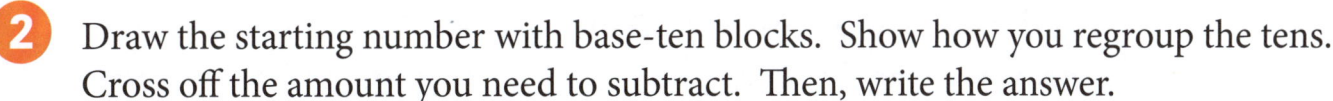

SUBTRACTION

2 Draw the starting number with base-ten blocks. Show how you regroup the tens. Cross off the amount you need to subtract. Then, write the answer.

```
  6 3
- 3 5
-----
  2 8
```
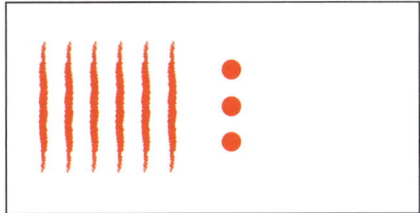  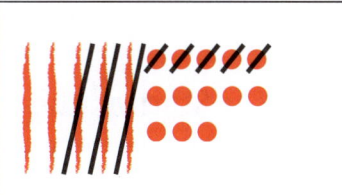

a
```
  5 4
- 2 6
```

b
```
  3 2
- 1 5
```

c
```
  4 6
- 2 9
```

d
```
  3 3
- 1 8
```

e
```
  3 6
- 1 7
```

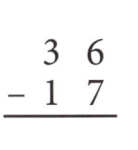  

SUBTRACTION

Standard Subtraction Algorithm

An algorithm is a strategy that follows the same steps each time you use it. You can use a standard algorithm to solve subtraction problems.

Step 1: Start at the ones place. You don't have enough ones in the top number to subtract the bottom. Regroup. Borrow a 10 from the tens place.

Step 2: Add the regrouped tens to the ones.

Step 3: Subtract the ones. Subtract the remaining tens.

```
  tens ones
    4  14
    5̸   4̸
  − 2   6
  ─────────
    2   8
```

The answer is **28**.

1 Use the standard algorithm to subtract. Show how you regroup. Write the answer.

```
    3 15
    4̸ 5̸
  − 1 9
  ──────
    2 6
```

a

```
    5 3
  − 2 9
  ──────
```

126 146444—Catch-Up Math   © Shell Education

Practice

SUBTRACTION

1 Look at how the tens have been regrouped. Solve each problem.

$$\begin{array}{r} ^{3}^{17} \\ \cancel{4}\,\cancel{7} \\ -1\,9 \\ \hline \mathbf{2\,8} \end{array}$$

e
$$\begin{array}{r} ^{4}^{15} \\ \cancel{5}\,\cancel{5} \\ -3\,6 \\ \hline \end{array}$$

a
$$\begin{array}{r} ^{3}^{14} \\ \cancel{4}\,\cancel{4} \\ -2\,5 \\ \hline \end{array}$$

f
$$\begin{array}{r} ^{4}^{12} \\ \cancel{5}\,\cancel{2} \\ -2\,6 \\ \hline \end{array}$$

b
$$\begin{array}{r} ^{6}^{13} \\ \cancel{7}\,\cancel{3} \\ -5\,4 \\ \hline \end{array}$$

g
$$\begin{array}{r} ^{5}^{13} \\ \cancel{6}\,\cancel{3} \\ -1\,5 \\ \hline \end{array}$$

c
$$\begin{array}{r} ^{5}^{15} \\ \cancel{6}\,\cancel{5} \\ -2\,7 \\ \hline \end{array}$$

h
$$\begin{array}{r} ^{7}^{15} \\ \cancel{8}\,\cancel{5} \\ -1\,7 \\ \hline \end{array}$$

d
$$\begin{array}{r} ^{6}^{12} \\ \cancel{7}\,\cancel{2} \\ -3\,8 \\ \hline \end{array}$$

i
$$\begin{array}{r} ^{5}^{16} \\ \cancel{6}\,\cancel{6} \\ -3\,7 \\ \hline \end{array}$$

SUBTRACTION

2 Use the standard algorithm to subtract. When needed, show how you regroup.

●
```
   3 12
   4̶ 2̶
 - 2 8
 ─────
   1 4
```

a
```
   6 6
 - 3 9
 ─────
```

b
```
   5 3
 - 1 2
 ─────
```

c
```
   7 5
 - 5 0
 ─────
```

d
```
   6 7
 - 4 9
 ─────
```

e
```
   5 1
 - 2 2
 ─────
```

f
```
   5 3
 - 2 9
 ─────
```

g
```
   4 7
 - 2 9
 ─────
```

h
```
   5 4
 - 3 0
 ─────
```

i
```
   4 4
 - 1 6
 ─────
```

SUBTRACTION

Subtraction with Three-Digit Numbers

You can subtract three-digit numbers using the same strategies you used for two-digit numbers.

Example 1: Subtract the hundreds, tens, and ones separately. Remember, this strategy only works if the top digits are all greater than the bottom digits.

Hundreds: 400 − 100 = 300

       4 5 2
       − 1 2 1

Tens: 50 − 20 = 30

Ones: 2 − 1 = 1

Total: 300 + 30 + 1 = **331**

Example 2: Draw base-ten blocks. Regroup if needed. Subtract numbers by drawing *X*s over the blocks.

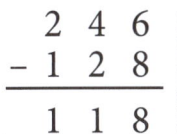

regroup a ten
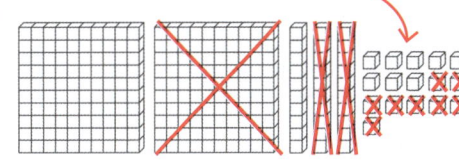

Example 3: Use the standard subtraction algorithm with three-digit numbers.

    6 13
  2 7̸ 3̸
  − 1 4 8
   1 2 5

Your turn

1 Solve the problem using the standard algorithm.

    3 11
  2 4̸ 1̸
 − 1 2 7
  1 1 4

> Make sure to line up the numbers by place value.

a 6 7 3
  − 2 3 8

SELF CHECK   Mark how you feel

Got it!    Need help...    I don't get it

Check your answers — How many did you get correct?

SUBTRACTION

Practice

1 Draw each starting number with base-ten blocks. Show how you regroup. Cross off the amount you must subtract. Then, write the answer.

●
```
  2 3 5
- 1 1 8
-------
  1 1 7
```

a
```
  3 3 3
- 1 1 7
```

b
```
  4 4 2
- 1 2 6
```

c
```
  2 6 4
- 1 3 8
```

2 Solve hundreds, tens, and ones separately. Write the missing numbers for each equation. Then, write the final answer.

● 257 − 113 = ?

Hundreds: **200** − **100** = **100**

Tens: **50** − **10** = **40**

Ones: **7** − **3** = **4**

Total: **100** + **40** + **4** = **144**

b 624 − 412 = ?

Hundreds: ___ − ___ = ___

Tens: ___ − ___ = ___

Ones: ___ − ___ = ___

Total: ___ + ___ + ___ = ___

a 356 − 221 = ?

Hundreds: ___ − ___ = ___

Tens: ___ − ___ = ___

Ones: ___ − ___ = ___

Total: ___ + ___ + ___ = ___

c 482 − 351 = ?

Hundreds: ___ − ___ = ___

Tens: ___ − ___ = ___

Ones: ___ − ___ = ___

Total: ___ + ___ + ___ = ___

SUBTRACTION

3 Look at how the tens have been regrouped. Write the answer to each problem.

⬤
```
      4 16
    2 5̶ 6̶
  - 1 3 8
  ───────
    1 1 8
```

a
```
      7 14
    3 8̶ 4̶
  - 2 1 7
  ───────
```

b
```
      2 17
    3 3̶ 7̶
  - 2 1 9
  ───────
```

c
```
      7 12
    6 8̶ 2̶
  - 3 4 6
  ───────
```

d
```
      4 15
    5 5̶ 5̶
  - 2 2 7
  ───────
```

e
```
      1 15
    4 2̶ 5̶
  - 2 1 6
  ───────
```

4 Use the standard algorithm to subtract. Show how you regroup, if needed.

⬤
```
      3 15
    2 4̶ 5̶
  - 1 3 6
  ───────
    1 0 9
```

a
```
    7 7 2
  - 4 2 6
  ───────
```

b
```
    5 2 7
  - 3 1 8
  ───────
```

c
```
    3 8 8
  - 2 7 9
  ───────
```

d
```
    5 8 1
  - 3 4 2
  ───────
```

e
```
    7 7 3
  - 5 4 6
  ───────
```

Subtraction Review

1 Count back to subtract.

a 22 − 4 = _____

b 36 − 8 = _____

c 54 − 5 = _____

d 78 − 6 = _____

e 31 − 4 = _____

f 28 − 7 = _____

g 43 − 8 = _____

h 58 − 3 = _____

i
```
  3 6
− 3 5
─────
```

j
```
  4 9
−   6
─────
```

k
```
  2 7
−   7
─────
```

l
```
  3 3
−   4
─────
```

m
```
  8 6
−   5
─────
```

n
```
  3 8
−   3
─────
```

Review

SUBTRACTION

2 Write the subtraction equations that are shown.

a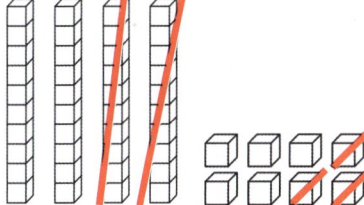

___ - ___ = ___

e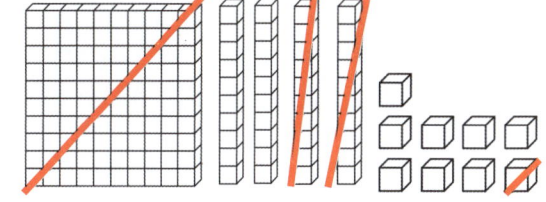

___ - ___ = ___

b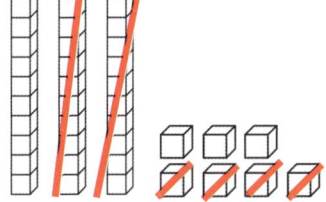

___ - ___ = ___

f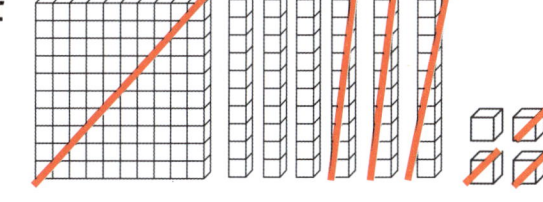

___ - ___ = ___

c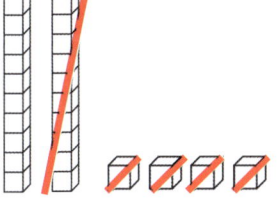

___ - ___ = ___

g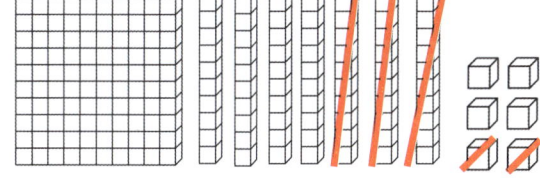

___ - ___ = ___

d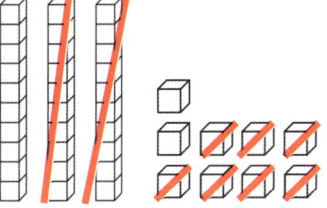

___ - ___ = ___

h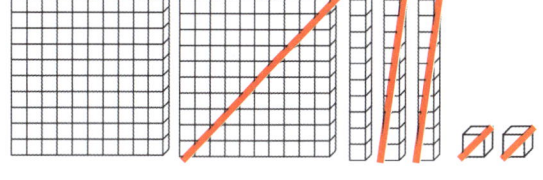

___ - ___ = ___

SUBTRACTION Review

3 Use the number line to solve each problem. Show your jumps. Write the answer.

a 13 − 5 = _____

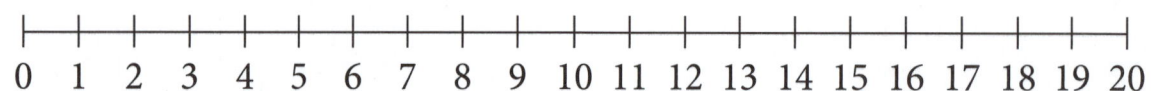

b 15 − 7 = _____

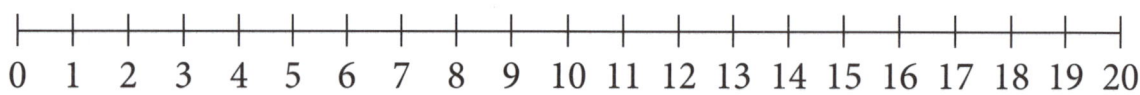

c 16 − 6 = _____

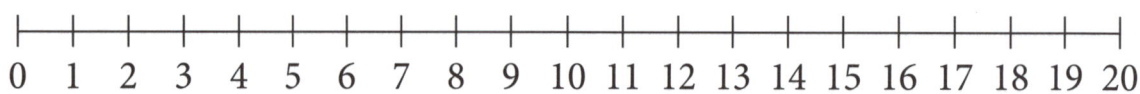

d 15 − 8 = _____

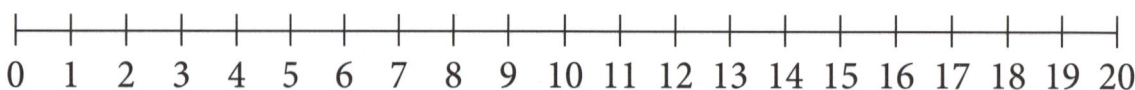

e 54 − 12 = _____

f 65 − 14 = _____

g 48 − 13 = _____

Review

SUBTRACTION

4 Solve the unknown addend problem first. Then, solve the subtraction problem.

a 18 – 9

9 + _____ = 18

18 – 9 = _____

b 16 – 7

7 + _____ = 16

16 – 7 = _____

c 20 – 12

12 + _____ = 20

20 – 12 = _____

d 15 – 8

8 + _____ = 15

15 – 8 = _____

e 12 – 6

6 + _____ = 12

12 – 6 = _____

f 14 – 6

6 + _____ = 14

14 – 6 = _____

5 Solve each subtraction problem.

a 9 + 6 = 15, so 15 – 9 = _____

b 8 + 10 = 18, so 18 – 8 = _____

c 11 + 5 = 16, so 16 – 11 = _____

d 6 + 8 = 14, so 14 – 8 = _____

e 5 + 8 = 13, so 13 – 5 = _____

f 15 + 7 = 22, so 22 – 15 = _____

SUBTRACTION

Review

 Subtract using the standard algorithm. The regrouping has been done for you.

a
```
   4 14
   5̸ 4̸
 − 2 5
```

c
```
   3 14
   4̸ 4̸
 − 2 6
```

b
```
   5 13
   6̸ 3̸
 − 2 6
```

d
```
   4 13
   5̸ 3̸
 − 2 7
```

 Subtract using the standard algorithm.

a
```
   6 4
 − 2 7
```

d
```
   6 4
 − 5 5
```

b
```
   7 3
 − 5 9
```

e
```
   2 8 7
 − 1 3 9
```

c
```
   3 7
 − 1 8
```

f
```
   1 4 3
 − 1 2 6
```

DATA AND GRAPHS

Charts

Data is information. Charts are used to display data.

Example 1: This table shows the data collected to answer this question: What is the favorite ice cream flavor of the students in Room 8?

This is the title of the chart.
It says what the data is showing.
↓

Room 8's Favorite Ice Cream Flavors

Flavor	Tally	Total
vanilla	|||||	5
chocolate	|||||		6
strawberry	|||	3
chocolate chip	||||| |||	8

These are tally marks. They show how many students voted for each flavor.

The total is the amount of tally marks.

Here are some of the things that we can learn from this chart:

- Chocolate chip is the most popular flavor.
- Strawberry is the least popular flavor.
- There is data for 22 total students.
- Two more students prefer chocolate chip over chocolate.

DATA AND GRAPHS

1 Count the tally marks. Record the totals.

Goals Scored by Victor's Soccer Team

Game	Tally	Total
1st Game	|||	3
2nd Game	||||/	
3rd Game	||	
4th Game		
5th Game	||	
6th Game			

Data can be shown in pictures, numbers, or symbols.

2 Use the chart to complete the sentences.

• The most goals that were scored in a game were ___5___.

a The game with no goals scored was the _____ game.

b The team scored 2 goals in the _____ and _____ games.

c The team scored _____ total goals in all 6 games.

SELF CHECK Mark how you feel
Got it!   Need help...   I don't get it

Check your answers
How many did you get correct?

Practice

DATA AND GRAPHS

1 Write the missing data in the chart.

Room 10's Favorite Types of Books

Type of Book	Tally	Total
fiction	IIII	4
animal facts	IIII I	
mystery		2
adventure		1
sports	III	3
comics	IIII I	6
science	IIII	

2 Complete the sentences, and answer the questions. Use the data from chart.

● The most popular type of book was __comics__.

a   The least popular type of book was _____.

b   The two types of books with the same votes were _____ and _____ books.

c   A total of _____ students in Room 10 voted.

d   How many more students prefer comics over adventure books?

_____

e   How many more students prefer science books over mystery books?

_____

f   How many students like sports and fiction books? _____

© Shell Education   146444—Catch-Up Math   **139**

DATA AND GRAPHS

3 Write the missing data in the chart.

Room 22's Favorite School Lunches

Type of Lunch	Tally	Total
pizza	llll llll	8
taco	lll	
chicken sandwich		1
noodles		3
peanut butter and jelly sandwich	lll	3
burrito	llll	4
fish sticks	ll	

4 Complete the sentences, and answer the questions. Use the data from the chart.

● The most popular school lunch is ___pizza___.

a The least popular school lunch was _____.

b Which lunches got 3 votes? _____, _____, and _____.

c A total of _____ students in Room 22 voted.

d How many more students prefer pizza over fish sticks? _____

e How many more students prefer burritos over tacos? _____

f How many students like noodles or chicken sandwiches? _____

DATA AND GRAPHS

Picture Graphs

A picture graph uses pictures to show data. A key tells you what the pictures mean.

Sunny Days

November	☀ ☀ ☀ ☀ ☀ ☀
December	☀ ☀
January	☀ ☀
February	☀ ☀ ☀
March	☀ ☀ ☀ ☀ ☀
April	☀ ☀ ☀ ☀ ☀ ☀ ☀

Key: ☀ = 1 day

The key says that 1 ☀ stands for 1 day.

April has 7 suns. This means there were 7 days in April that were sunny. December and January had the fewest sunny days.

Your turn

1 Look at the picture graph. It shows the favorite sports of second graders. Use it to answer the questions.

Key: ⭐ = 1 student

Favorite Sports in Room 2

football	⭐ ⭐ ⭐ ⭐ ⭐ ⭐ ⭐
baseball	⭐ ⭐ ⭐ ⭐ ⭐
soccer	⭐ ⭐ ⭐ ⭐ ⭐
hockey	⭐

● How many students like football?

7 students

a Which sport was chosen by 1 student?

_____

SELF CHECK Mark how you feel
Got it! | Need help… | I don't get it

Check your answers
How many did you get correct?

DATA AND GRAPHS

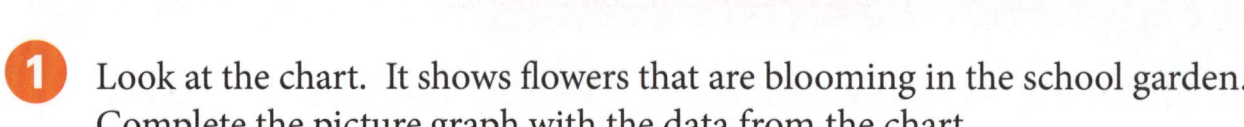

1 Look at the chart. It shows flowers that are blooming in the school garden. Complete the picture graph with the data from the chart.

Flowers in the School Garden

Flowers	Total Votes
tulip	IIII
rose	IHI I
lily	I
iris	III

Flowers in the School Garden

tulip	🌷 🌷 🌷 🌷
rose	
lily	
iris	

Key: 🌷 = 1 flower

2 Answer the questions. Use the data from the picture graph.

● How many roses are blooming?

__6 roses__

a Which flower has 3 blooming?

_____

b How many more roses are blooming than lilies?

_____

c How many tulips and irises are blooming?

_____

d How many flowers are blooming all together?

_____

e Which type of flower has the most flowers blooming?

_____

142   146444—Catch-Up Math   © Shell Education

DATA AND GRAPHS

3 Look at the chart. It shows students' favorite pets. Complete the picture graph with the data from the chart.

Students' Favorite Pets

Favorite Pets	Total
dog	6
cat	8
hamster	2
rabbit	3

Students' Favorite Pets

dog	♥ ♥ ♥
cat	
hamster	
rabbit	♥ ♥

Key: ♥ = 2 students

4 Answer the questions. Use the data from the picture graph.

● How many students like dogs best?
  <u>6 students</u>

a Which is the least popular pet?
  _____

b How many more students like cats than hamsters?
  _____

c Which pet is prefered by 2 students?
  _____

d How many students like rabbits best?
  _____

DATA AND GRAPHS

5 Students shared their favorite recess activities. The data is listed in the chart. Use it to complete the picture graph.

Students' Favorite Recess Activities

Activity	Total
swings	5
baseball	3
monkey bars	3
tag	2

Students' Favorite Recess Activities

swings	★ ★ ★ ★ ★
baseball	
monkey bars	
tag	

Key: ★ = 1 student

6 Answer the questions. Use the data from the picture graph.

● How many students like swings the most?

   <u>5 students</u>

a Which is the least popular activity?

   _____

b How many more students like baseball than tag?

   _____

c Which activity is preferred by 2 students?

   _____

d How many students voted in all?

   _____

DATA AND GRAPHS

Bar Graphs

A bar graph shows data in bars. The bars may be vertical (up and down) or horizontal (side to side).

Example 1: A bar graph can be vertical.

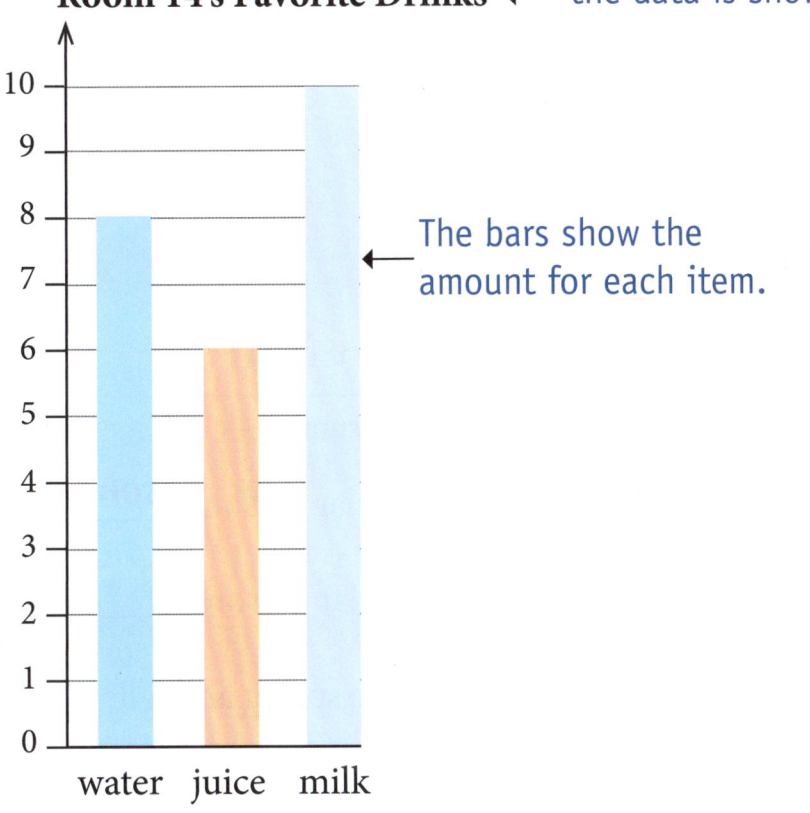

The title tells what the data is showing.

The bars show the amount for each item.

Example 2: A bar graph can be horizontal. This graph shows the same data as the vertical graph. Draw the missing bar.

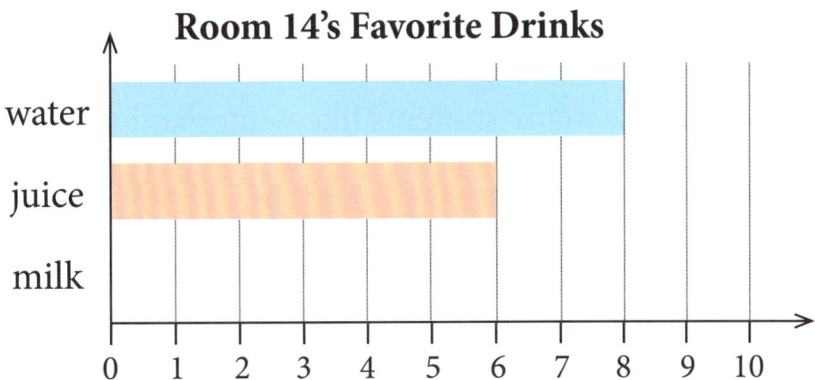

DATA AND GRAPHS

1 Use the bar graph to answer the questions.

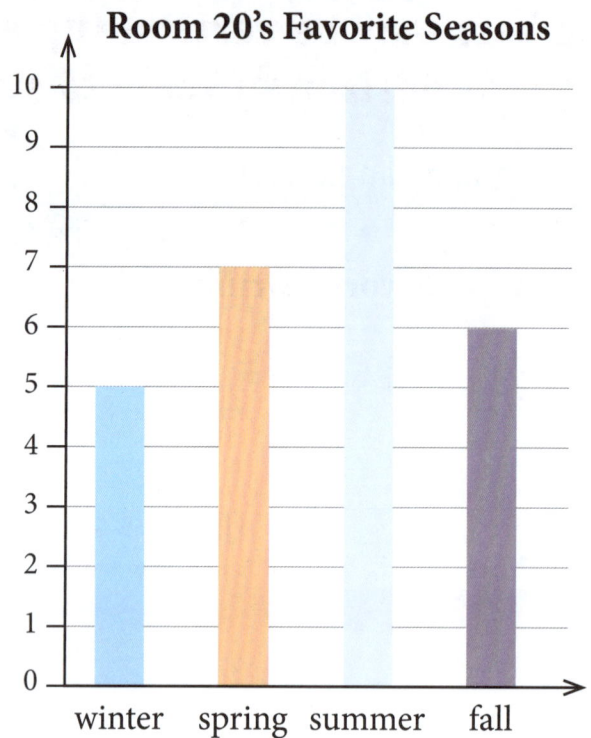

When you make a bar graph, make sure your bars stop at the right spots!

● Which is the most popular season? __summer__

a Which is the least popular season? _____

b How many students like spring and fall? _____

c How many more students like summer than winter? _____

d How many more students like spring than fall? _____

e How many students like winter and summer? _____

f How many students voted? _____

Practice

DATA AND GRAPHS

1 Use the bar graph to answer the questions.

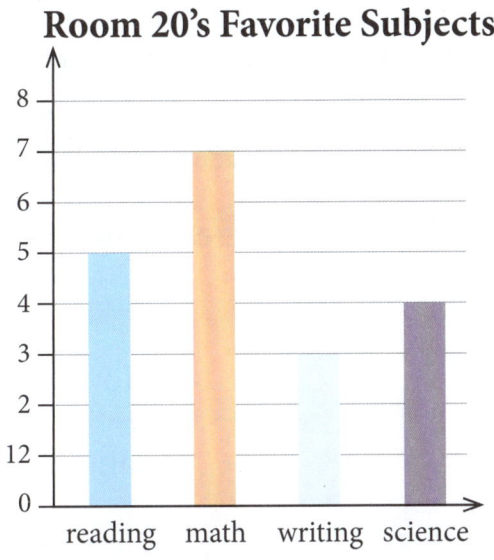

● Which subject is the most popular?

    math

a Which subject is the least popular?

_____

b How many students like science and writing?

_____

c How many more students like reading than science?

_____

d How many more students like math than writing?

_____

e How many students like reading, science, or writing?

_____

f How many students voted?

_____

2 Complete the table. Use the data from the bar graph above.

Room 18's Favorite Subjects

Favorite Subjects	Tally Marks	Total
reading	|||||	
math		7
writing	|||	
science		4

DATA AND GRAPHS

3 Look at the bar graph. Answer the questions.

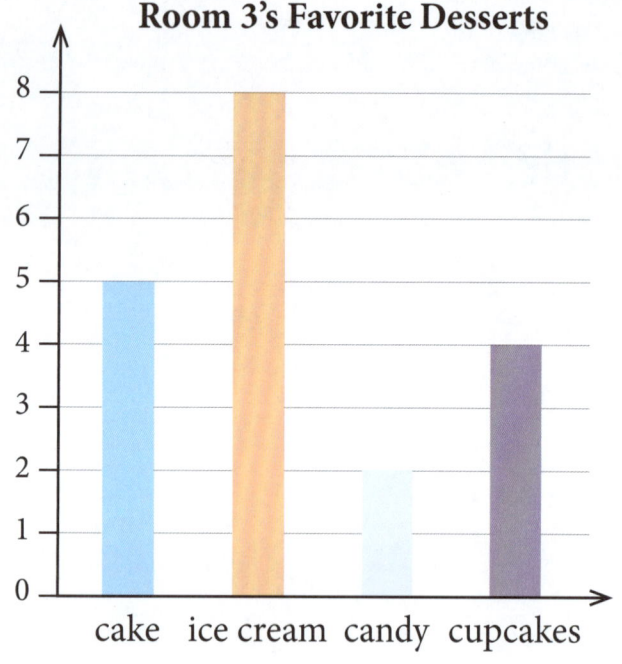

● Which dessert is the most popular?

ice cream

a Which dessert is the least popular? _____

b How many students like cake or candy? _____

c How many more students like ice cream than candy? _____

d How many students like ice cream or cake? _____

e How many students voted? _____

4 Complete the bar graph with the same data as above.

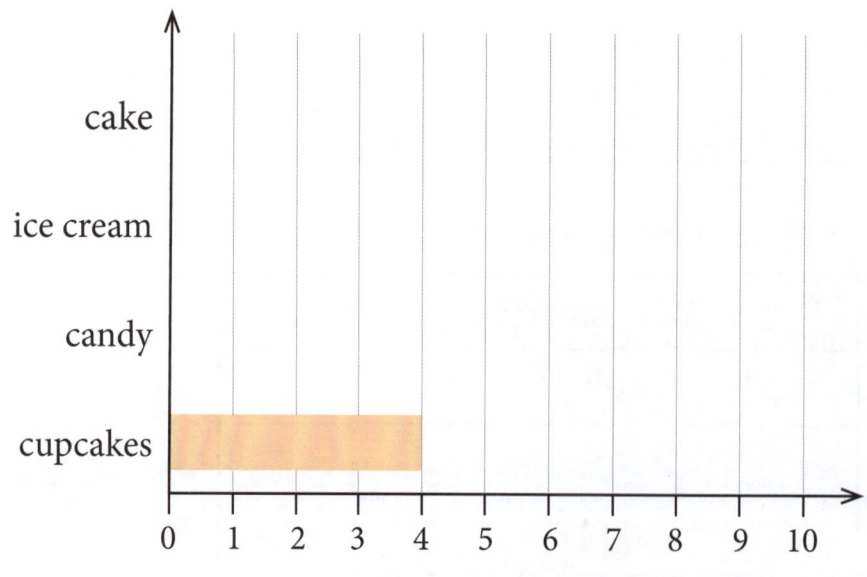

Room 3's Favorite Desserts

DATA AND GRAPHS

5 Complete the bar graph to show the data. Be sure to add a title.

Room 12's Favorite Days

Day	Total
Sunday	3
Monday	1
Tuesday	0
Wednesday	2

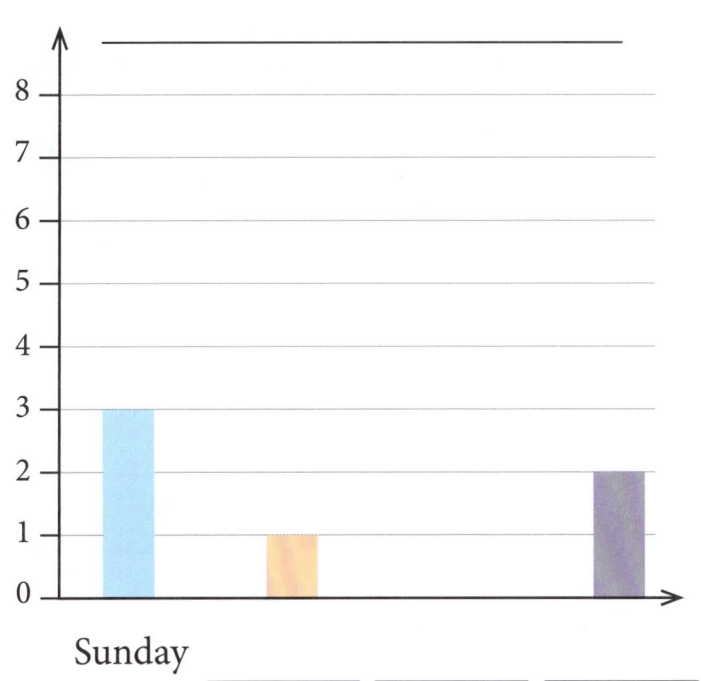

Sunday _____ _____ _____

6 Write questions you could ask about the data. Write the answers.

• Question: **How many students voted for Wednesday?**

Answer: **2 students**

a Question: _____

Answer: _____

b Question: _____

Answer: _____

7 What kind of data would you like to collect and show in a bar graph?

_____

_____

DATA AND GRAPHS

Line Plots

A line plot shows data on a number line.

Example 1: Look at this table. It shows the lengths of different pencils.

Pencil	Length (inches)
A	3
B	3
C	4
D	2
E	3
F	5

Pencil A is 3 inches long. The other pencils (B, C, D, E, and F) are listed, too. You can show this data on a line plot.

Lengths of Pencils

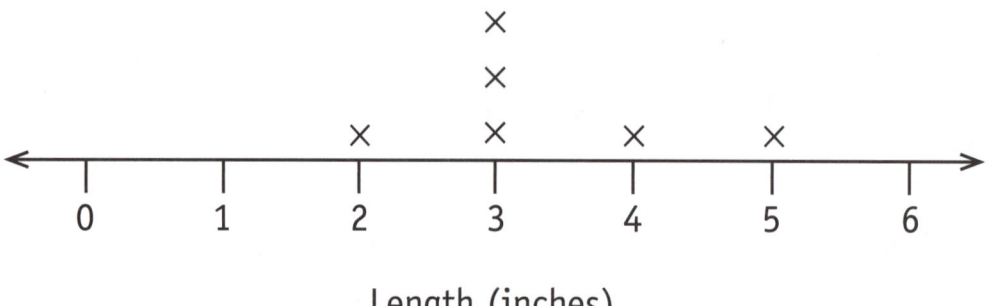

Length (inches)

The line plot is on a number line. It shows the lengths of the pencils. Each *X* is 1 pencil. Notice that above the 3, there are 3 *X*s. That means there are 3 pencils that are 3 inches long.

DATA AND GRAPHS

Your turn

1 Look at the chart. Add the data from the chart to the line plot.

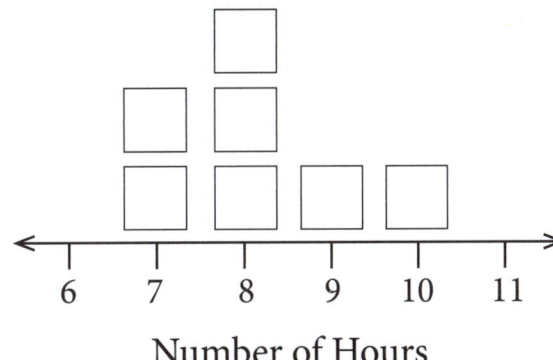

Hours Carlos Slept	
Night	Hours
Sunday	8
Monday	7
Tuesday	9
Wednesday	8
Thursday	7
Friday	10
Saturday	8

Make all your Xs the same size on a line plot.

2 Use the line plot to answer the questions.

● How many nights did Carlos sleep 7 hours?

   2 days

   a How many nights did Carlos sleep 11 hours?

   _____

   b How many nights did Carlos sleep 9 or 10 hours?

   _____

   c How many more nights did Carlos sleep 8 hours than he slept 9 hours?

   _____

SELF CHECK Mark how you feel
Got it!   Need help...   I don't get it

Check your answers
How many did you get correct?

DATA AND GRAPHS

Practice

1 Paulo baked blueberry muffins. He kept track of how many blueberries were in each muffin. Use the chart to complete the line plot.

Blueberries in Muffins

Muffin	Number of Blueberries
A	4
B	5
C	6
D	4
E	5
F	7
G	6
H	5

Blueberries in Muffins

1 2 3 4 5 6 7 8

Number of Muffins

2 Answer questions using the data from the line plot in question 1.

How many muffins have 4 blueberries? **2 muffins**

a Why are there no Xs above 1, 2, and 3? _____

b How many muffins had 5 blueberries? _____

c What was the greatest amount of blueberries in a muffin? _____

d What was the least amount of blueberries in a muffin? _____

e How many muffins did Paulo bake? _____

DATA AND GRAPHS

3 Simon's soccer team runs laps at practice. The chart lists how many laps each player ran. Make a line plot using the data.

Laps Players Ran at Soccer Practice

Player	Laps
A	5
B	3
C	4
D	4
E	5
F	3
G	3
H	2

_____

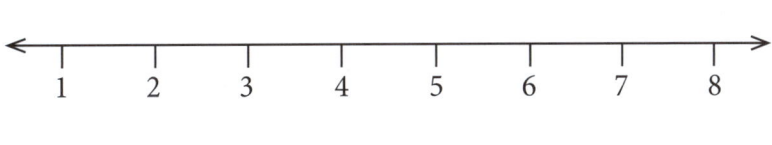

_____

4 Answer these questions using the data from the graph.

● How many players ran 4 laps? **2 players**

a How many players ran 5 laps? _____

b How many players ran 3 laps? _____

c What was the least amount of laps ran? _____

d What was the most amount of laps ran? _____

e How many players ran 2 or 3 laps? _____

DATA AND GRAPHS

5 This chart shows how many books these students read in a week. Make a line plot with the data from the chart.

Books Read in a Week

Student	Number of Books
Jose	2
Lin	1
Phoebe	4
Laila	4
Ivan	3
Luke	2
Oscar	2
Maya	3

_____

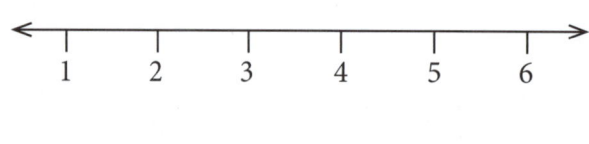

_____

6 Write questions you could ask about the data. Write the answers.

● Question: **What was the greatest number of books read?**

Answer: **4 books**

a Question: _____

Answer: _____

b Question: _____

Answer: _____

Data and Graphs Review

DATA AND GRAPHS

1 Look at the chart. Make a bar graph with the data.

Room 15's Favorite Animals

Animals	Tally Marks	Total
panda	IIII	4
giraffe	IIII	4
tiger	III	3
wolf	IIII II	7

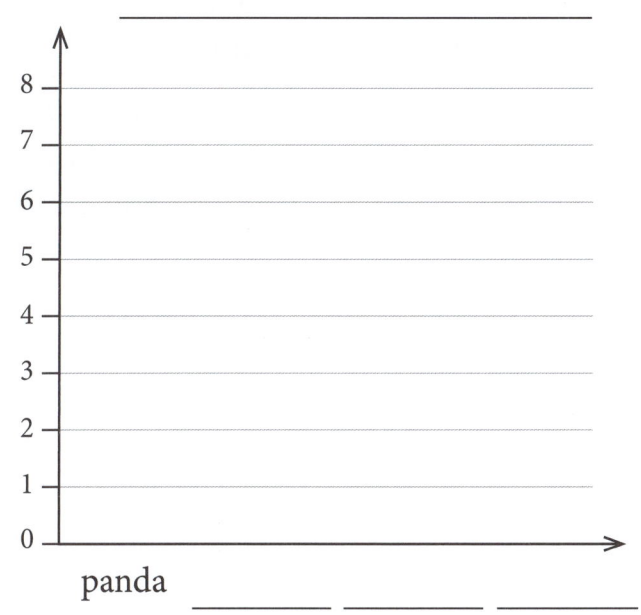

2 Use your bar graph to answer the questions.

a   Which is the most popular animal? _____

b   Which is the least popular animal? _____

c   How many students like pandas? _____

d   How many students like tigers or giraffes? _____

3 Write 2 more questions that you can answer with the bar graph. Write the answers.

a   Question: _____

   Answer: _____

b   Question: _____

   Answer: _____

DATA AND GRAPHS

Review

4 The chart shows what the students in Room 1 like to do for Choice Time. Make a picture graph to show the data.

Room 1's Choice Time Activities

Choice Time Activity	Total
drawing	3
blocks	6
computers	3
reading	4

Room 1's Choice Time Activities

drawing	
blocks	
computers	
reading	

Key: ♥ = 1 student

5 Write two questions that you can ask about this data. Write the answers.

a Question: _____

Answer: _____

b Question: _____

Answer: _____

Review

DATA AND GRAPHS

6 Sunny goes to an after-school club. The chart shows the ages of the children at the club. Make a line plot using the data.

Children at the After-School Club

Child	Age
A	5
B	6
C	6
D	7
E	5
F	8
G	6
H	7

_____

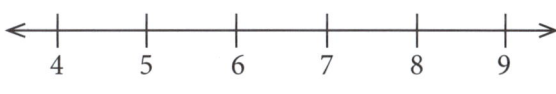

_____

7 Use the line plot to answer these questions.

a How many children at the club are 5 years old? _____

b How many children at the club are 6 years old? _____

c What age is the oldest child? _____

d Why are 4 and 9 blank with no Xs? _____

e What age are the youngest children? _____

DATA AND GRAPHS

Review

8 The chart shows how many syllables are in each student's name. Complete a bar graph to show the data.

Syllables in Names

Name	Total Syllables
Greta	2
Emma	2
Jack	1
Carolina	4

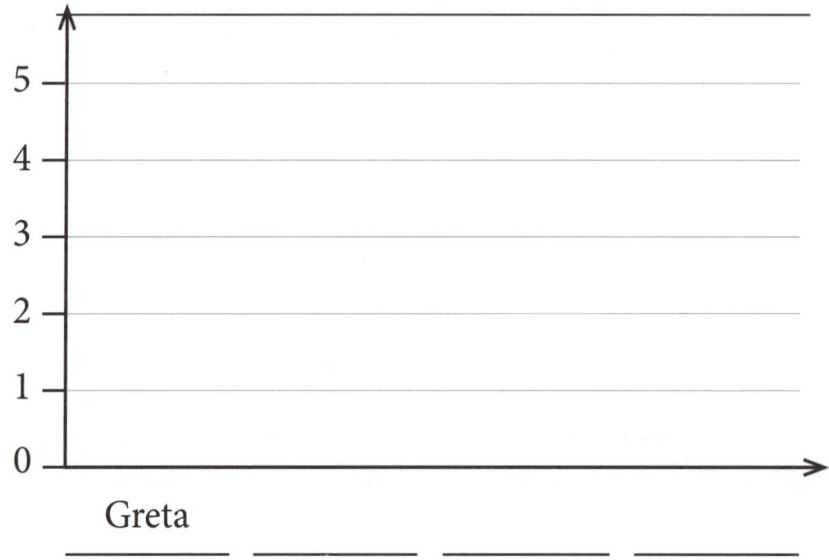

Greta _____ _____ _____ _____

Shape Attributes

An attribute is the way you describe a shape. It might be its size, color, number of sides, or number of vertices.

△ △ △ A triangle has 3 sides and 3 vertices.

☐ ☐ ▱ ▱ A quadrilateral has 4 sides and 4 vertices.

⬠ A pentagon has 5 sides and 5 vertices.

⬡ A hexagon has 6 sides and 6 vertices.

☐ A square has 4 **equal** sides and 4 square vertices.

These are the attributes that define these shapes.

Your turn

1 Color the triangles blue. Color the quadrilaterals green. Color the pentagons red. Color the hexagons yellow.

Some attributes do not define a shape, such as color or size.

SELF CHECK Mark how you feel
- Got it!
- Need help...
- I don't get it

Check your answers
How many did you get correct?

SHAPES AND ARRAYS

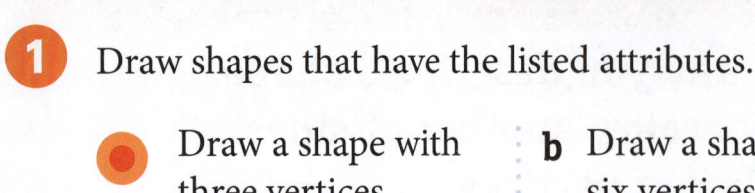

1. Draw shapes that have the listed attributes.

   • Draw a shape with three vertices.

   b Draw a shape with six vertices.

   d Draw a shape with four equal sides.

   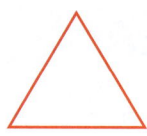

   a Draw a shape with four sides.

   c Draw a shape with five sides.

   e Draw a shape with four vertices.

2. Draw shapes that have the listed attributes.

   • Draw a red quadrilateral.

   b Draw a large green pentagon.

   d Draw a small orange rectangle.

   a Draw a small blue triangle.

   c Draw a small purple hexagon.

   e Draw a large yellow square.

SHAPES AND ARRAYS

Make New Shapes

You can compose, or make, new shapes from 2 or more two-dimensional shapes.

Example 1: A two-dimensional shape is flat. It has 2 measurements: length and width.

Example 2: If you put these shapes together, they make something new. The new shape is a composite shape.

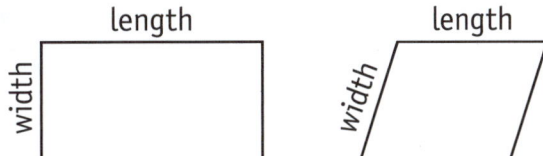

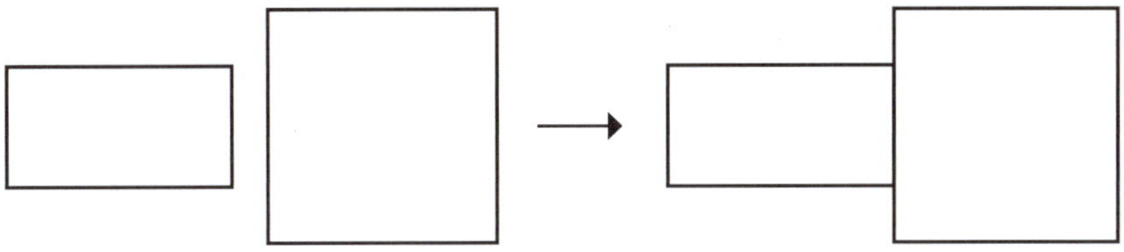

Your turn

1. Look at each pair of shapes. Draw one new shape using the two shapes.

• ▷ ◁ ▭   ◁═══

You can make more than one composite shape. They can be put together in different ways.

a.

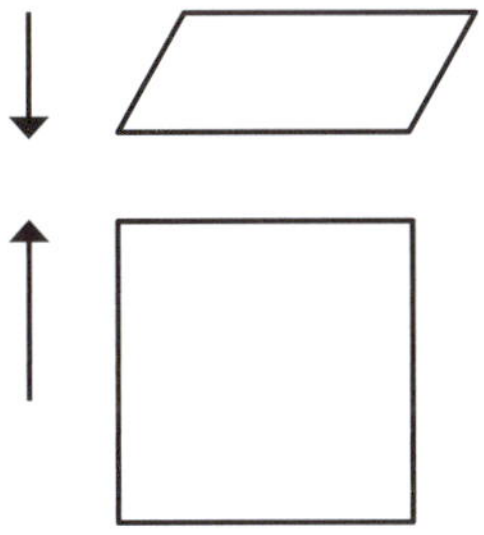

SELF CHECK Mark how you feel
Got it!   Need help...   I don't get it

Check your answers
How many did you get correct?

SHAPES AND ARRAYS

Practice

1 What two shapes do you see in each figure? Color them with different colors.

● What shapes do you see in this quadrilateral?

 two triangles

a What shapes do you see in this rectangle?

_____

b What shapes do you see in the figure?

_____

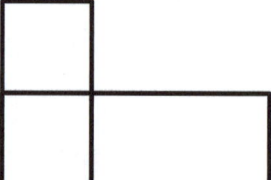

c What shapes do you see in the hexagon?

_____

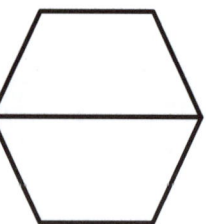

d What shapes do you see in the trapezoid?

_____

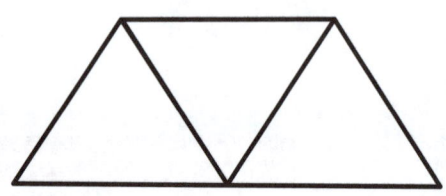

Practice

SHAPES AND ARRAYS

2 Look at each pair of shapes. Draw one new shape using each set of shapes.

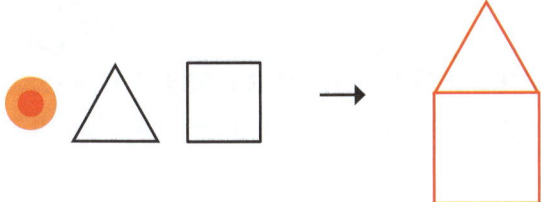

a

b

c

d

e

3 Draw a house using shapes. Make sure it has a roof, a door, and windows.

SHAPES AND ARRAYS

Understanding Arrays

An array is a way to arrange objects into rows and columns. It is arranged in the shape of a rectangle or a square.

Example 1: This array has 2 rows. It has 4 columns. There are 8 hearts.

Example 2: This array has 3 rows. It has 5 columns. There are 15 boxes.

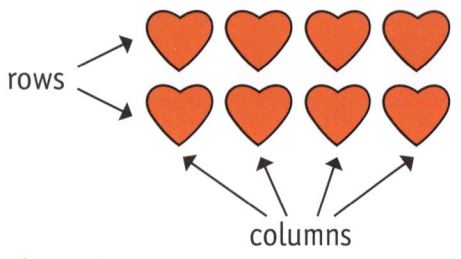

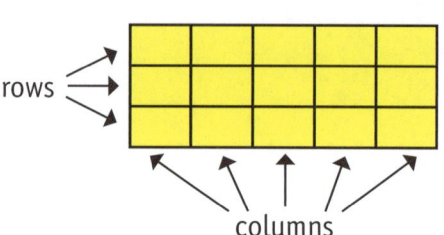

Your turn

 Write how many rows and columns are in each array. Write how many total objects are in each array.

___3___ rows

___3___ columns

___9___ total stars

a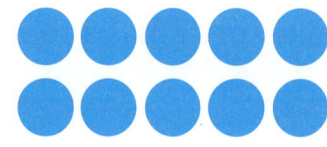

_____ rows

_____ columns

_____ total circles

Count each object of an array to find how many there are.

Check your answers
How many did you get correct?

Practice

SHAPES AND ARRAYS

1 Follow the directions to draw arrays. Use any shapes you want. Write the total number of objects for each array.

● Draw an array with 2 rows and 3 columns.

●●●
●●●

Total: **6**

d Draw an array with 4 rows and 3 columns.

Total: _____

a Draw an array with 4 rows and 4 columns.

Total: _____

e Draw an array with 4 rows and 2 columns.

Total: _____

b Draw an array with 5 rows and 2 columns.

Total: _____

f Draw an array with 3 rows and 4 columns.

Total: _____

c Draw an array with 5 rows and 3 columns.

Total: _____

g Draw an array with 2 rows and 6 columns.

Total: _____

SHAPES AND ARRAYS

Arrays with Rectangles

You can partition shapes into rows and columns. This will make a number of same-size parts.

Rows go across.

Columns go up and down.

This rectangle is split into 4 rows and 3 columns.

Example 1: You can partition this shape into 2 rows and 4 columns. Then, count to find how many squares there are.

Step 1: Draw one horizontal line in the middle. This makes 2 rows.
Step 2: Draw 3 vertical lines. This makes 4 columns.
Step 3: Count the squares.

Try to space your rows and columns evenly!

There are **8** squares in this rectangle.

Your turn

1 Partition the rectangles as described.

• 2 rows, 3 columns

a   4 rows, 3 columns

SELF CHECK Mark how you feel
Got it!   Need help...   I don't get it

Check your answers
How many did you get correct?

166 146444—Catch-Up Math   © Shell Education

Practice

SHAPES AND ARRAYS

1 Partition each rectangle as described. Then, count how many parts are in the rectangle. Write the total.

● 5 rows, 2 columns

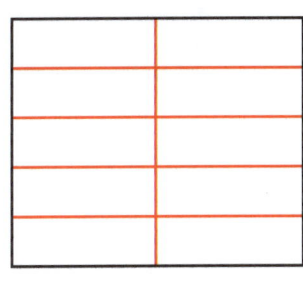

___10___ parts

c 4 rows, 4 columns

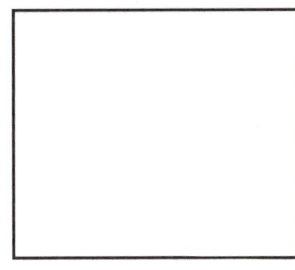

_____ parts

a 3 rows, 4 columns

_____ parts

d 5 rows, 3 columns

_____ parts

b 2 rows, 5 columns

_____ parts

e 4 rows, 2 columns

_____ parts

SHAPES AND ARRAYS

Add Arrays

You can add to find the number of objects in an array.

Example 1: This array has 2 rows and 3 columns.

You can add the rows. 3 + 3 = **6**

You can also add the columns. 2 + 2 + 2 = **6**

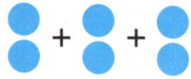

Example 2: This array has 2 rows and 5 columns.

You can add the rows. 5 + 5 = **10**

You can also add the columns. 2 + 2 + 2 + 2 + 2 = **10**

When you add arrays by rows or by columns, you get the same answer!

 **Your turn**

1 Use the arrays to add. Add the rows. Write the answers.

  ___2___ + ___2___ = ___4___

a  ____ + ____ + ____ = ____

b  ____ + ____ = ____

SELF CHECK Mark how you feel
Got it!   Need help...   I don't get it

Check your answers
How many did you get correct?

Practice

SHAPES AND ARRAYS

1 Study the arrays. Add the rows. Then, add the columns.

Rows: __3__ + __3__ = __6__

Columns: __2__ + __2__ + __2__ = __6__

a Rows: ____ + ____ + ____ = ____

Columns: ____ + ____ + ____ = ____

b Rows: ____ + ____ + ____ + ____ + ____ = ____

Columns: ____ + ____ = ____

c

Rows: ____ + ____ = ____

Columns: ____ + ____ + ____ + ____ + ____ + ____ = ____

d

Rows: ____ + ____ + ____ + ____ + ____ = ____

Columns: ____ + ____ + ____ = ____

e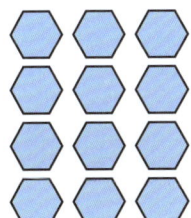

Rows: ____ + ____ + ____ + ____ = ____

Columns: ____ + ____ + ____ = ____

Shapes and Arrays Review

1 Look at the shapes. Combine them in different ways to make 6 new shapes.

△ triangle   ▭ rectangle   ⬡ hexagon

□ square   ⏢ trapezoid

a

b

c

d

e

f

2 Partition each rectangle as described. Then, count how many parts are in the rectangle. Write the total.

a 5 rows, 2 columns

total _____

b 3 rows, 3 columns

total _____

Review

SHAPES AND ARRAYS

3 Draw arrays with the given rows and columns. Use any shapes.

a   2 rows, 4 columns

c   4 rows, 3 columns

b   1 row, 5 columns

d   2 rows, 5 columns

4 Add the rows of each array. Then, add the columns.

a

Rows: _____ + _____ + _____ = _____

Columns: _____ + _____ + _____ + _____ + _____ + _____ = _____

b

Rows: _____ + _____ = _____

Columns: _____ + _____ = _____

c

Rows: _____ + _____ + _____ + _____ + _____ = _____

Columns: _____ + _____ + _____ + _____ = _____

d

Rows: _____ + _____ + _____ = _____

Columns: _____ + _____ = _____

FRACTIONS

Equal Parts

A shape can be divided into equal parts. That means all the parts of the shape are the same size.

Example 1: These shapes are divided into 2 equal parts, or halves.

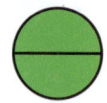 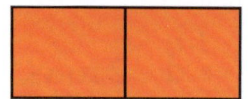

SCAN to watch video

Example 2: These shapes are divided into 3 equal parts, or thirds.

Example 3: These shapes are divided into 4 equal parts, or fourths.

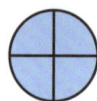 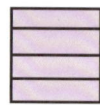

Example 4: These shapes are not divided into equal parts.

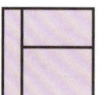 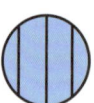 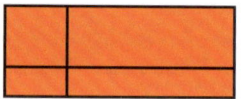

Your turn

1 Label the equal parts.

  _thirds_

a   _____

b 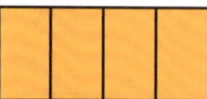 _____

c  _____

Look closely to make sure that parts are equal in size!

SELF CHECK Mark how you feel

Got it!  ☐   Need help...  ☐   I don't get it  ☐

Check your answers
How many did you get correct?

Practice

FRACTIONS

1 Circle the shapes divided into equal parts.

• Circle the shapes divided into halves.

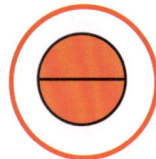 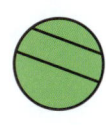 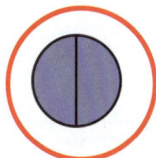 

a Circle the shapes divided into thirds.

  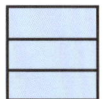 

b Circle the shapes divided into halves.

 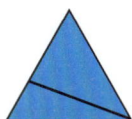  

c Circle the shapes divided into fourths.

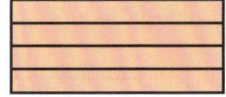 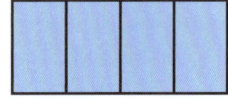 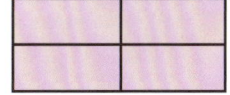 

2 Draw lines to divide the shapes. Make sure the parts are equal.

a Divide the shapes into halves.

 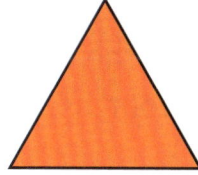  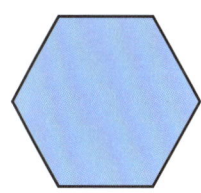

b Divide the shapes into thirds.

 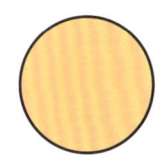 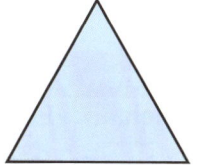 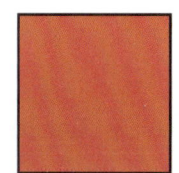

FRACTIONS

Partition Rectangles

Rectangles can be divided into equal parts in different ways.

Example 1: A rectangle can be divided into two equal parts, or halves, in different ways.

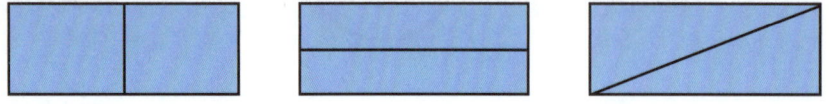

Example 2: A rectangle can be divided into three equal parts, or thirds, in different ways.

Example 3: A rectangle can be divided into four equal parts, or fourths, in different ways.

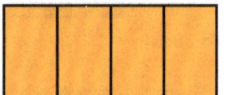 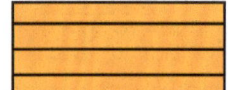 

1 Divide each rectangle as described.

-  Divide the rectangle into halves.

a  Divide the rectangle into fourths.

b 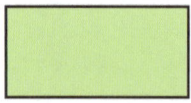 Divide the rectangle into thirds.

The divided parts of a shape are always smaller than the whole shape.

SELF CHECK Mark how you feel

Got it!  Need help...  I don't get it

Check your answers
How many did you get correct?

Practice

FRACTIONS

1 Divide each set of rectangles in different ways.

● Divide the rectangles into halves.

a Divide the rectangles into thirds.

b Divide the rectangles into fourths.

2 Color the rectangles as described. Some rectangles will not be colored.

a Find the rectangles that are divided into halves. Color them blue.

b Find the rectangles that are divided into thirds. Color them red.

c Find the rectangles that are divided into fourths. Color them green.

  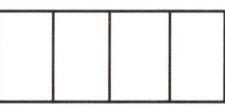

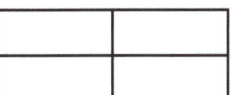  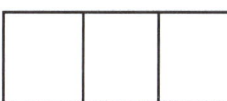

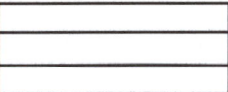 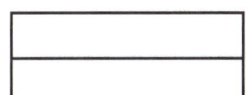 

FRACTIONS

Partition Circles

Circles can be divided into equal parts in different ways.

Example 1: These circles are divided into halves. It does not matter which way the dividing line goes.

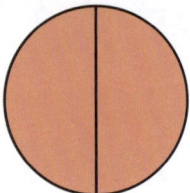 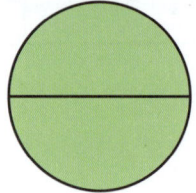

Example 2: These circles are divided into thirds. It does not matter which way the dividing lines go.

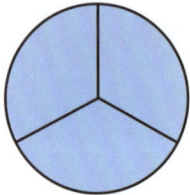 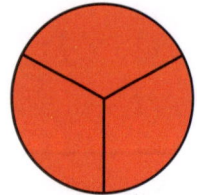

Example 3: These circles are divided into fourths. It does not matter which way the dividing lines go.

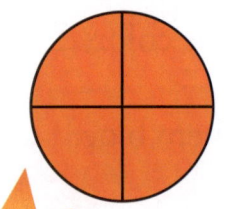 

Your turn

1. Write how each circle is divided.

 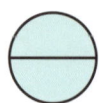 halves

a 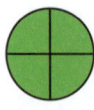 _____   b  _____

SELF CHECK Mark how you feel

Got it!   Need help...   I don't get it

Check your answers
How many did you get correct?

Practice

FRACTIONS

1 Divide each set of circles in different ways.

● Divide the circles into halves.

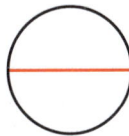 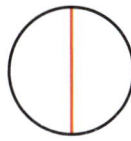

a Divide the circles into fourths.

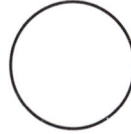 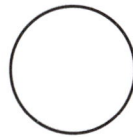

b Divide the circles into thirds.

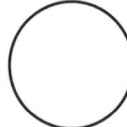 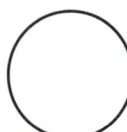

2 Color the circles as described. Some circles will not be colored.

a Find the circles that are divided into halves. Color them blue.

b Find the circles that are divided into thirds. Color them red.

c Find the circles that are divided into fourths. Color them green.

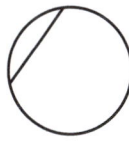   

  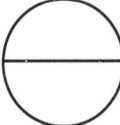 

FRACTIONS

Naming Fractions

You can describe how many equal parts of a whole are shaded.

Example 1:

 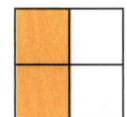  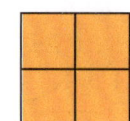

One-fourth of the shape is shaded.
Two-fourths of the shape is shaded.
Three-fourths of the shape is shaded.
Four-fourths of the shape is shaded. This means the whole shape is shaded.

Example 2: Use these fraction words to describe how many equal parts are shaded.

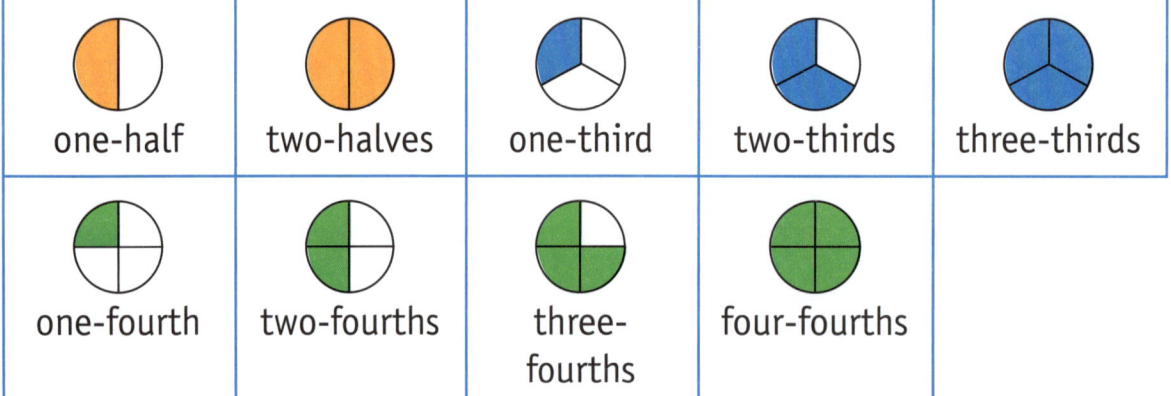

Your turn

1. How much of each shape is shaded?

  three-fourths

a 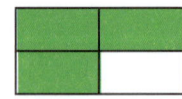 _____

SELF CHECK Mark how you feel
Got it! 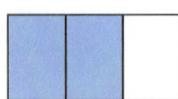 Need help...  I don't get it

Check your answers
How many did you get correct?

178 146444—Catch-Up Math   © Shell Education

Practice

FRACTIONS

1 Shade the shapes to show the fractions.

● three-fourths 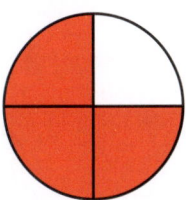   e one-half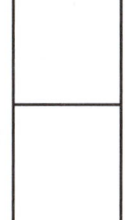

a one-half 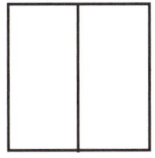   f three-fourths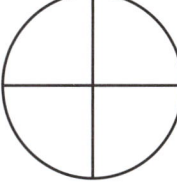

b two-thirds 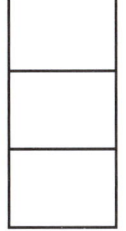   g two-halves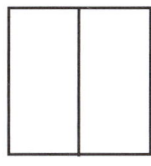

c one-third    h three-thirds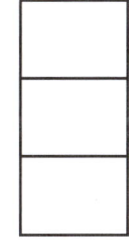

d two-fourths 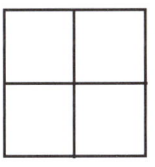   i four-fourths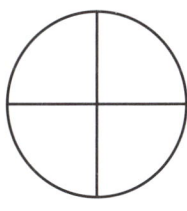

2 What pattern do you notice when whole shapes are shaded?

_____

_____

FRACTIONS **Practice**

3 Circle the correct shapes.

● Circle the shape with two-fourths shaded.

 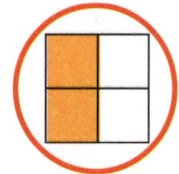 

c Circle the shape with two-halves shaded.

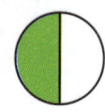  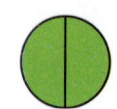

a Circle the shape with two-thirds shaded.

d Circle the shape with two-fourths shaded.

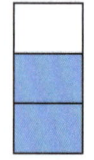 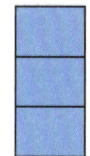 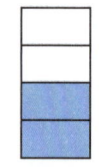

b Circle the shape with two-thirds shaded.

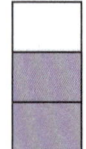 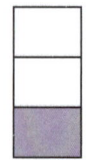 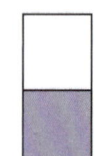

e Circle the shape with one-third shaded.

 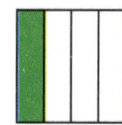 

4 How much of each shape is shaded?

● 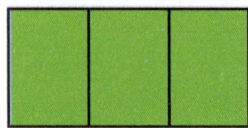   *three-thirds*

a 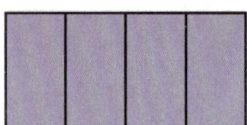   _____

b 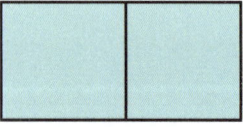   _____

Fractions Review

FRACTIONS

1 Color the shapes as described. Some shapes may not be colored.

a Find the shapes that are divided into halves. Color them red.

b Find the shapes that are divided into thirds. Color them green.

c Find the shapes that are divided into fourths. Color them blue.

 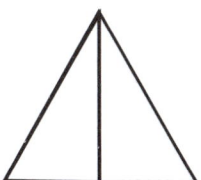 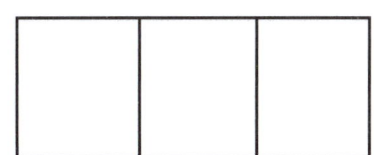

 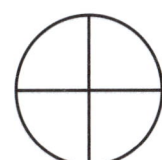 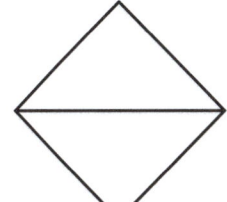

 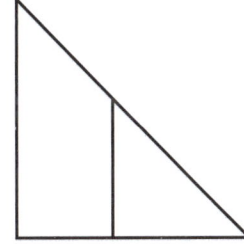 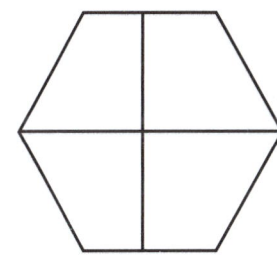

 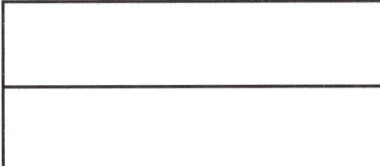 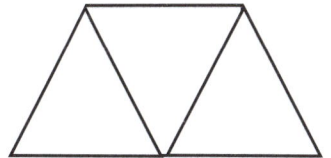

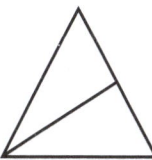  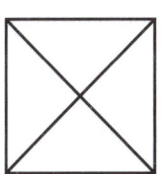

FRACTIONS Review

2 Divide the shapes as described.

  a Divide each shape into halves.

    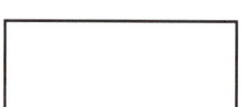 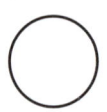

  b Divide each shape into thirds.

    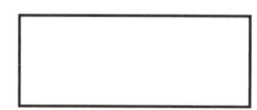 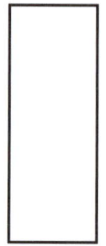

  c Divide each shape into fourths.

3 Shade the shapes as described.

  a Shade three-fourths of the shape.

  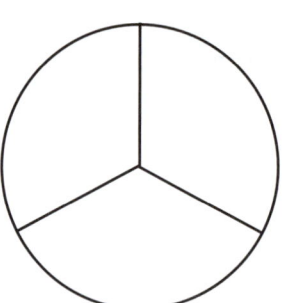

  c Shade two-thirds of the shape.

  b Shade two-halves of the shape.

  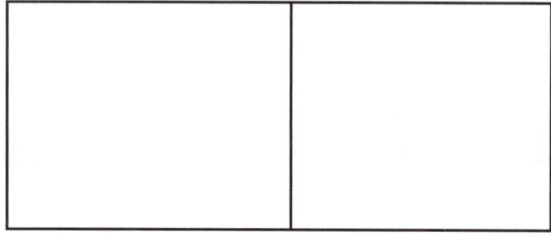

  d Shade one-fourth of the shape.

  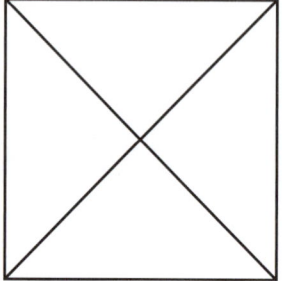

182   146444—Catch-Up Math   © Shell Education

Review

FRACTIONS

 Complete each shape as described.

a Draw a rectangle. Divide it into halves. Shade one-half.

b Draw a square. Divide it into fourths. Shade three-fourths.

c Draw a rectangle. Divide it into thirds. Shade one-third.

d Draw a square. Divide it into thirds. Shade two-thirds.

e Draw a rectangle. Divide it into fourths. Shade one-fourth.

f Draw a square. Divide it into halves. Shade two-halves.

g Draw a rectangle. Divide it into fourths. Shade two-fourths.

LENGTH

Measurement Tools

Different tools can be used to measure an object's length, or how long it is.

A ruler is a measurement tool. It usually measures something in inches or centimeters.

A yardstick is another tool. It measures something around one yard long. This is the same as 3 feet.

A measuring tape can be used to measure in inches or centimeters. It can measure very large things.

Your turn

1. Circle the word that matches each picture.

ruler   (yardstick)   measuring tape

a.

ruler   yardstick   measuring tape

b.

ruler   yardstick   measuring tape

Using the right measurement tool gives you the most accurate measurement.

SELF CHECK Mark how you feel
Got it!   Need help...   I don't get it

Check your answers
How many did you get correct?

Practice

LENGTH

1 Circle the tool you would use to measure each object.

(ruler)
yardstick
measuring tape

d
ruler
yardstick
measuring tape

a
ruler
yardstick
measuring tape

e
ruler
yardstick
measuring tape

b
ruler
yardstick
measuring tape

f
ruler
yardstick
measuring tape

c
ruler
yardstick
measuring tape

g
ruler
yardstick
measuring tape

LENGTH

2 Circle the best unit of measurement to use for each object.

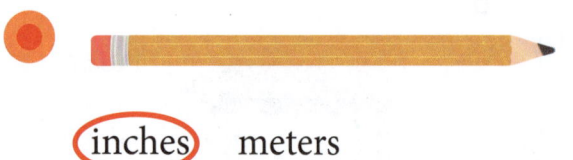

(inches)   meters

e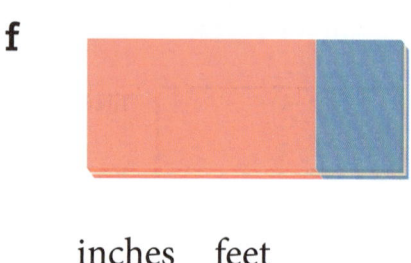

centimeters   yards

a

centimeters   yards

f

inches   feet

b

inches   meters

g

feet   centimeters

c

centimeters   feet

h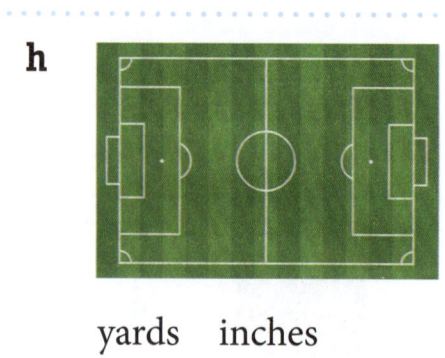

yards   inches

d

centimeters   meters

i

centimeters   meters

LENGTH

Measurement Units

You can measure the same object with different units of measurement.

Example 1: This pen is about 12 base-ten blocks long. It is also 7 cubes long.

SCAN to watch video

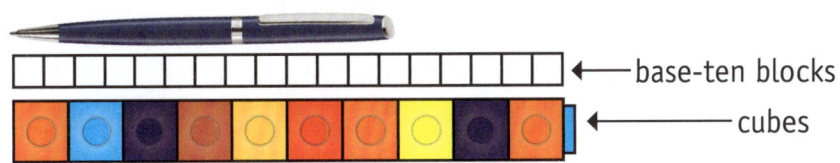
← base-ten blocks
← cubes

Example 2: This pen cap is 2 inches long. It is also 5 centimeters long.

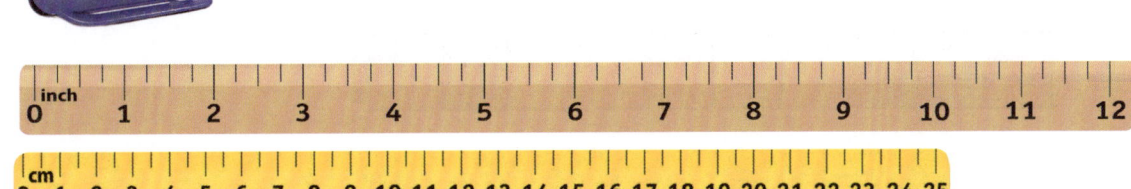

Your turn

1 Measure the objects with cubes and base-ten blocks.

If the measurement is not exact, list the one it is closest to.

__12__ base-ten blocks

__7__ cubes

The cubes are bigger than base-ten blocks. That is why it takes fewer to make the length of the scissors.

a

_____ base-ten blocks

_____ cubes

SELF CHECK Mark how you feel

Got it!   Need help...   I don't get it

Check your answers
How many did you get correct?

© Shell Education

146444—Catch-Up Math

187

LENGTH

Practice

1 Measure the objects with cubes and base-ten blocks.

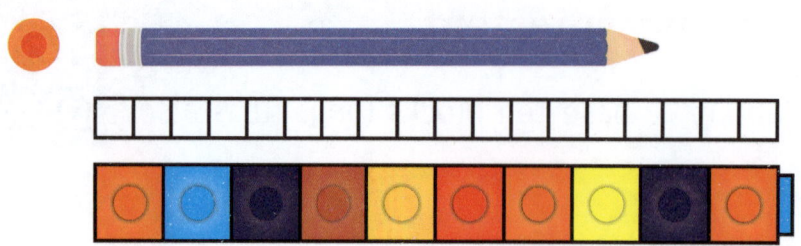

_15_ base-ten blocks

_8_ cubes

a

_____ base-ten blocks

_____ cubes

b

_____ base-ten blocks

_____ cubes

c

_____ base-ten blocks

_____ cubes

d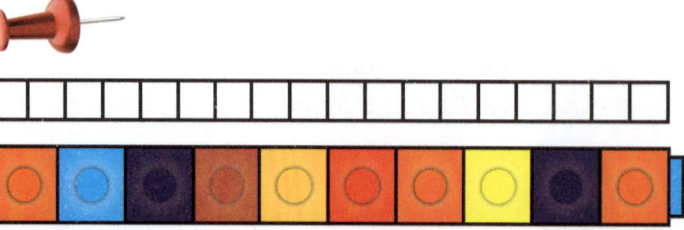

_____ base-ten blocks

_____ cubes

2 Measure the objects in inches and centimeters.

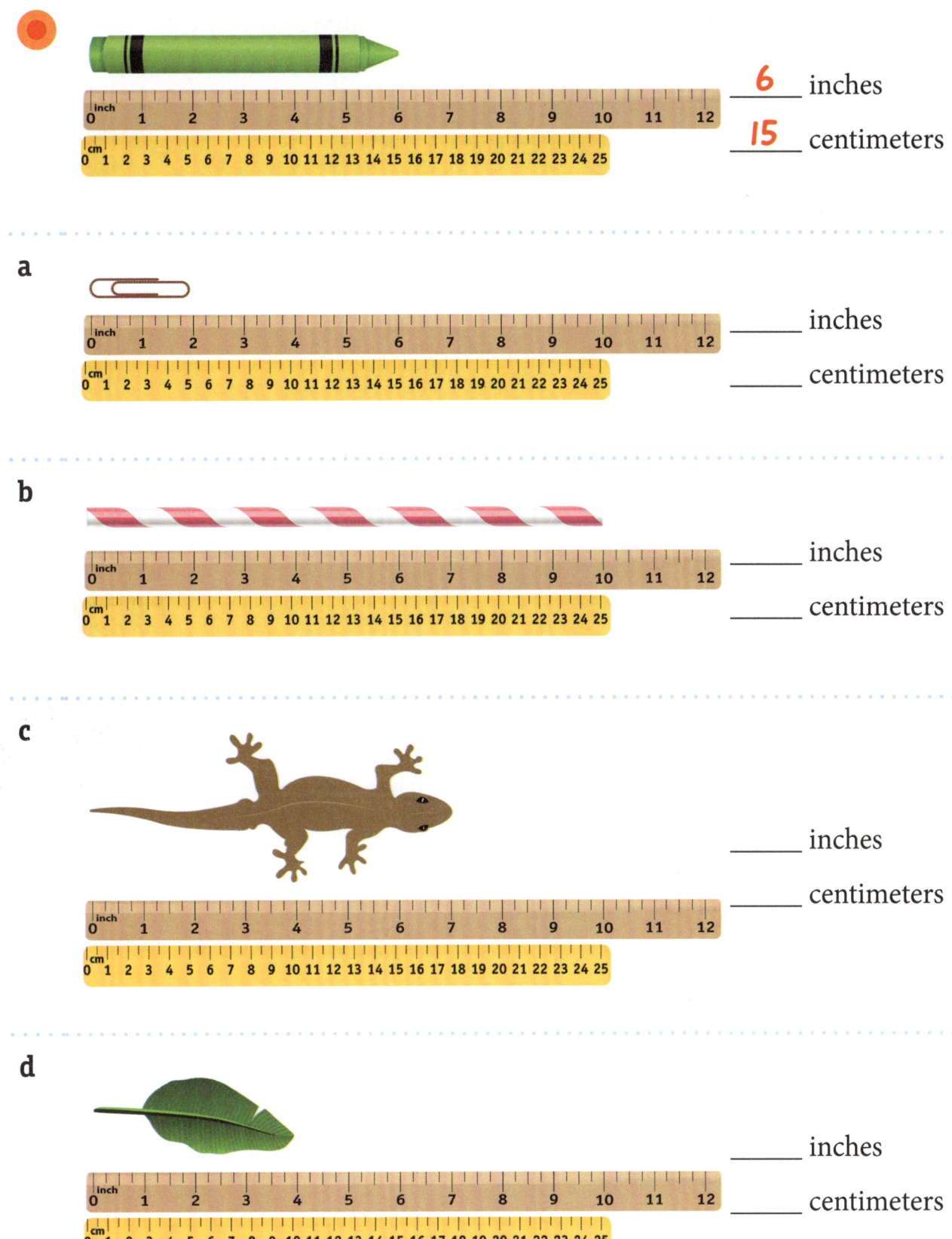

- _6_ inches
- _15_ centimeters

a) ____ inches / ____ centimeters

b) ____ inches / ____ centimeters

c) ____ inches / ____ centimeters

d) ____ inches / ____ centimeters

LENGTH

LENGTH

Inches and Centimeters

You can measure the lengths of things. You can measure in inches or centimeters.

Example 1: Look at the ruler. It is 1 inch from each number to the next.

How many inches long is the crayon?

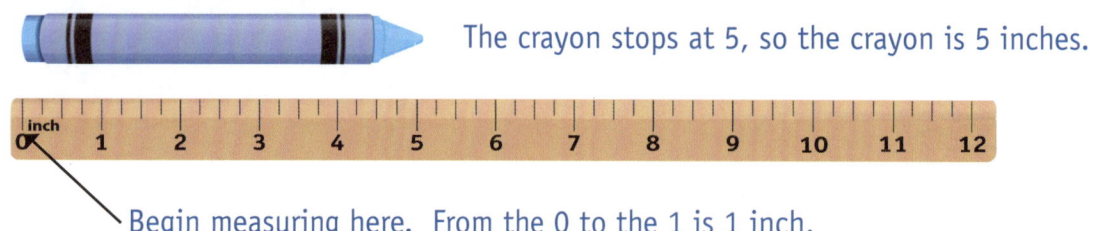

The crayon stops at 5, so the crayon is 5 inches.

Begin measuring here. From the 0 to the 1 is 1 inch.

Example 2: Look at the ruler. It is 1 centimeter from each number to the next.

How many centimeters long is the bug?

The bug is **3** centimeters long.

The shorter lines between the numbers measure parts of an inch or centimeter.

Your turn

1 Measure each line in inches.

____4____ inches

a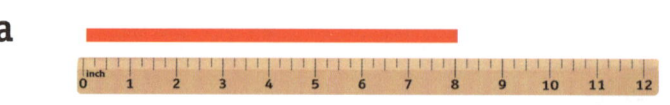

_____ inches

SELF CHECK Mark how you feel — Got it! / Need help... / I don't get it

Check your answers — How many did you get correct?

Practice

LENGTH

1 Measure each object in inches.

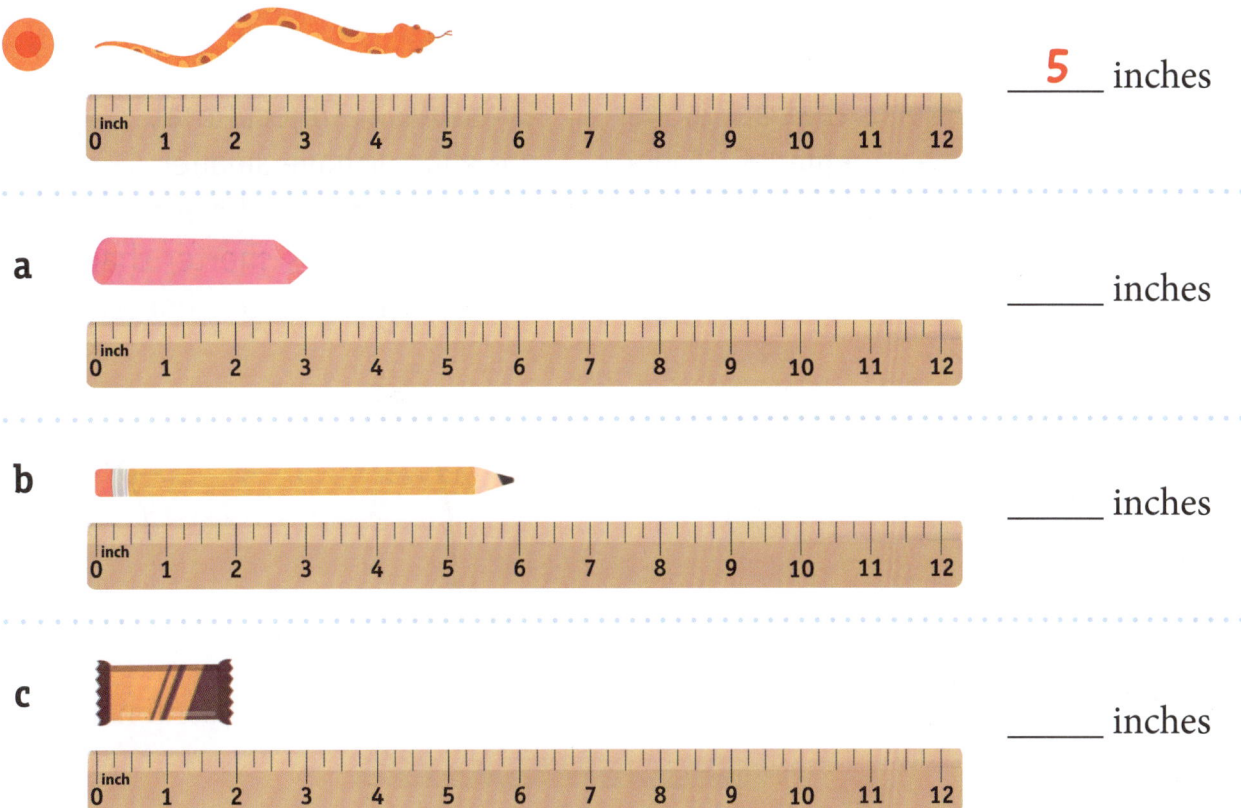

_____5_____ inches

a _____ inches

b _____ inches

c _____ inches

2 Measure each line in centimeters.

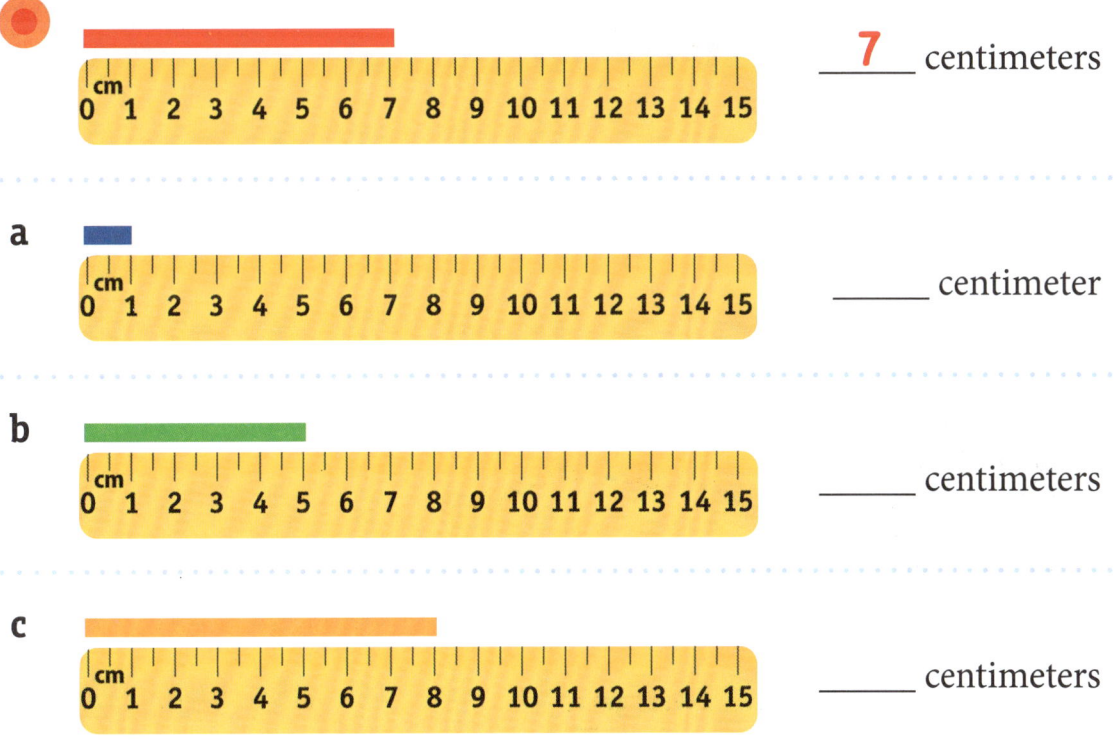

_____7_____ centimeters

a _____ centimeter

b _____ centimeters

c _____ centimeters

LENGTH

Compare Lengths

You can compare objects to see which object is shorter or longer.

Example 1: Objects that are longer have greater measurements. A book that is 10 inches is longer than a book that is 8 inches.

8 inches

10 inches

Example 2: Objects that are shorter have smaller measurements. A flower that is 6 centimeters is shorter than a flower that is 11 centimeters.

11 centimeters

6 centimeters

Your turn ① Look at each pair of objects. Complete the sentences.

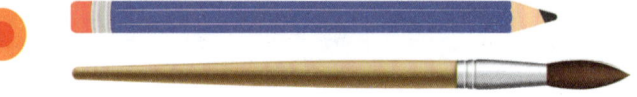

The ___pencil___ is shorter than the ___paintbrush___.

a

The _____ is longer than the _____.

Make sure objects are lined up at one end when you compare their lengths.

b

The _____ is shorter than the _____.

SELF CHECK Mark how you feel

Got it!   Need help...   I don't get it

Check your answers
How many did you get correct?

Practice

LENGTH

1 Circle the longer or taller object in each set.

c

a

d

b
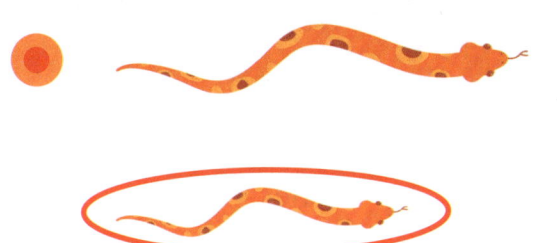

e

2 Circle the shorter object in each set.

c

a
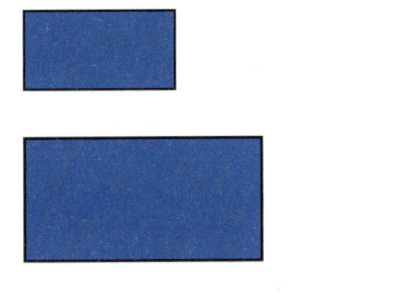

d
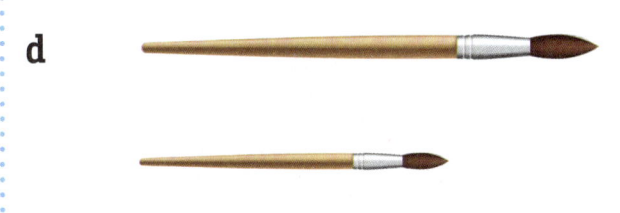

b

e

LENGTH

3 Answer the questions to compare the lengths.

How much longer is the ribbon?

__3__ inches longer

c How much longer is the blue pen?

_____ inches longer

a How much longer is the marker?

_____ inches longer

d How much longer is the pink candy?

_____ inches longer

b How much longer is the red fish?

_____ inches longer

e How much longer is the first candy bar?

_____ inches longer

LENGTH

Estimate Lengths

You can estimate a measurement. This means making your closest guess about how long an object is.

Making a good estimate means understanding *about* how long each unit is so you can make a guess about its length.

- One **centimeter** is about as long as a ladybug.
- One **inch** is about as long as a paper clip.
- One **foot** is as long as a ruler.
- One **yard** is as long as a yardstick or a baseball bat.
- One **meter** is about as long as a baseball bat.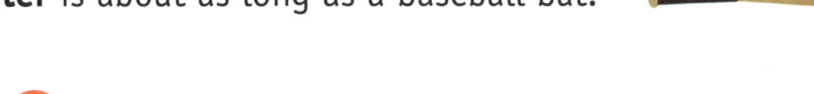

Your turn

1 Estimate the length or height of each object. Write the unit of measurement.

estimate: 7 __feet__

b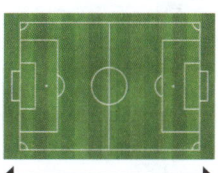

estimate: 100 _____

It is okay to make a guess when you estimate. Try to make a reasonable guess that could be close to the actual measurement.

a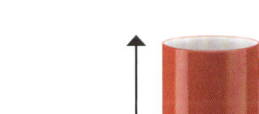

estimate: 4 _____

c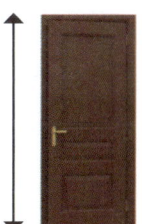

estimate: 2 _____

SELF CHECK Mark how you feel

Got it! 😀 ☐   Need help... 😐 ☐   I don't get it 😟 ☐

Check your answers
How many did you get correct?

195

LENGTH

Practice

1 Look at each object. Circle the best estimate for the length or height.

● (6 feet) 1 foot

c 15 meters   15 inches

a 18 inches   18 centimeters

d 1 yard   1 centimeter

b 10 inches   10 yards

e 7 inches   7 meters

2 Order the objects from longest to shortest. Write a 1 next to the longest object. Write a 3 next to the shortest object. Write a 2 next to the object in the middle by length.

● __1__ a car
   __2__ a shoe
   __3__ a pushpin

b _____ a desk
   _____ a playground slide
   _____ a sheet of notebook paper

a _____ a notebook
   _____ a nail
   _____ a doorway

c _____ a soccer ball
   _____ a fence
   _____ a crayon

Length Word Problems

You can solve word problems involving length measurements.

Example 1: Mia has 3 ribbons. The blue ribbon is 5 inches long, the red ribbon is 7 inches long, and the green ribbon is 6 inches long. How long are all 3 ribbons all together?

- What is this word problem asking? You have to add three numbers together.

5 + 7 + 6 = **18**

Your answer is 18 **inches** because the unit of measurement is in inches.

Example 2: Jayden kicked a soccer ball 20 feet. Liam kicked a soccer ball 10 feet. How much farther did Jayden kick the ball?

- What is this word problem asking? You have to subtract the numbers to find the difference.

20 − 10 = **10**

Your answer is 10 **feet** because the unit of measurement is in feet.

1. Write equations to solve the problems.

    James has two long chains of blocks. One chain is 25 inches. The other is 10 inches. How long are both blocks all together?

    25 + **10** = **35 inches**

    a Riley got a long piece of licorice. It was 14 inches long. She gave 7 inches of it to her sister. How many inches did she have left?

    _____ − _____ = _____

Read word problems carefully. Circle the numbers, and underline clue words, such as all together.

SELF CHECK Mark how you feel — Got it! / Need help... / I don't get it

Check your answers — How many did you get correct?

LENGTH

Practice

1 Read the word problems. Write equations to solve them.

 Amaya makes a bracelet that is 15 centimeters long. Lucy makes a bracelet that is 12 centimeters long. How long are the two bracelets together?

__15__ + __12__ = __27__ centimeters

a Mom bought 2 balloons for the party. One balloon has a string that is 25 inches long. The other balloon has a string that is 22 inches long. How many inches of string are there all together?

_____ _____ _____ = _____ inches

b Evan measured his frog's jumps. The first jump was 16 centimeters. The second jump was 9 centimeters. How much longer was the first jump?

_____ _____ _____ = _____ centimeters

c Two neighbors built a fence together. One section was 18 feet long. The other section was 15 feet long. How long was the fence in all?

_____ _____ _____ = _____ feet

d Luis played a football game. He ran 22 yards on his first play. He ran 14 yards on his second play. How far did he run in all?

_____ _____ _____ = _____ yards

e Sam ran in P.E. He ran 53 feet. Peter ran 37 feet. How much farther did Sam go?

_____ _____ _____ = _____ feet

f Chloe ran down the mat in gymnastics. She ran 27 feet and jumped. Then, she ran 14 feet. How much longer was her first run?

_____ _____ _____ = _____ feet

Length Review

LENGTH

1 Circle the best tool to measure each object.

a

    ruler
    yardstick
    measuring tape

c

    ruler
    yardstick
    measuring tape

b

    ruler
    yardstick
    measuring tape

d

    ruler
    yardstick
    measuring tape

2 Circle the best measurement unit for each object.

a

    inches   yards

c

    centimeters   feet

b

    centimeters   meters

d

    centimeters   meters

LENGTH Review

3 Draw each object.

a Draw something that is about 6 feet.

c Draw something that is about 2 yards.

b Draw something that is about 5 inches.

d Draw something that is about 3 centimeters.

4 Circle the longer or taller object in each set.

a

c

b

d

5 Circle the shorter object in each set.

a

c

b

d

Review

LENGTH

6 Complete the sentences. Choose objects around you.

a The _____ is shorter than the _____.

b The _____ is shorter than the _____.

7 Answer the questions to compare the lengths.

a How much longer is the orange snake?

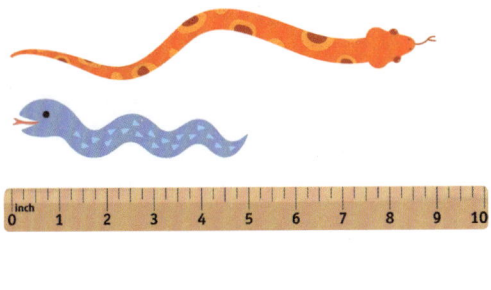

_____ inches longer

b How much longer is the needle?

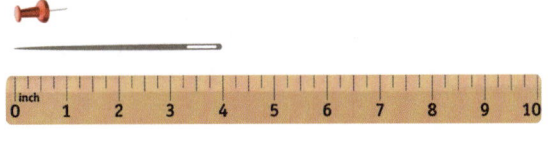

_____ inches longer

8 Look at each object. Circle the best estimate for its length.

a

6 inches   6 feet

b

8 inches   8 yards

c

14 feet   14 centimeters

d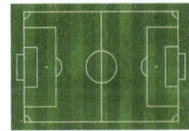

50 yards   50 inches

e

40 inches   40 feet

f

1 inch   1 meter

Review

9 Write the length of each object.

a

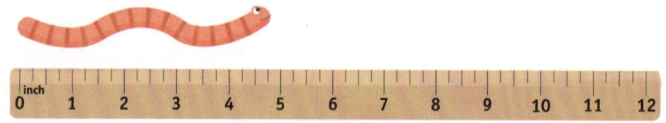

_____ inches

b

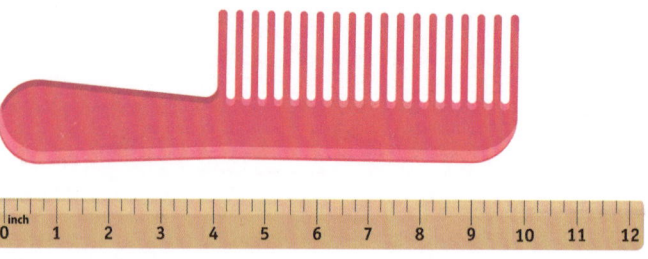

_____ inches

c

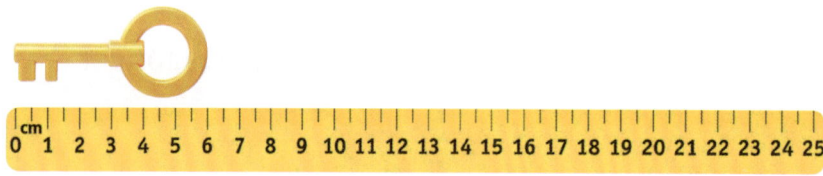

_____ centimeters

d

_____ centimeters

e

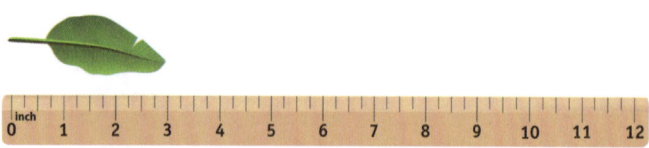

_____ inches

f

_____ inches

Review

LENGTH

10 Measure the objects in inches and centimeters.

a
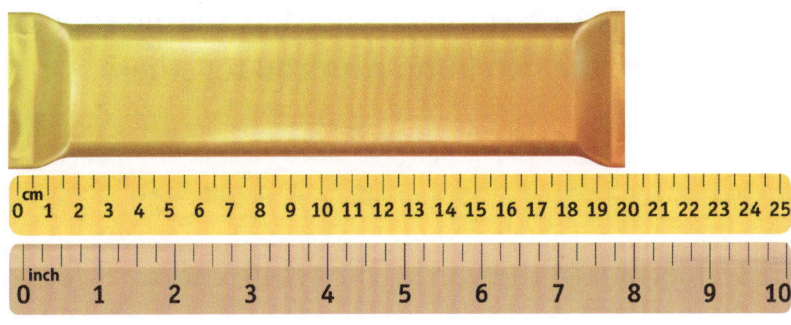

_____ centimeters

_____ inches

b

_____ centimeters

_____ inches

11 Measure the objects with cubes and base-ten blocks.

a

_____ base-ten blocks

_____ cubes

b

_____ base-ten blocks

_____ cubes

LENGTH Review

12 Read the word problems. Write equations to solve the problems.

a Lola has a jump rope that is 12 feet long. Alice has a jump rope that is 13 feet long. How long are the two jump ropes all together?

_____ _____ _____ = _____ feet

b The black cat ran 15 feet out of the yard. The white cat ran 9 feet out of the yard. How much farther did the black cat go?

_____ _____ _____ = _____ feet

c One ladybug moved 30 centimeters. Another ladybug moved 21 centimeters. How much farther did the first ladybug travel?

_____ _____ _____ = _____ centimeters

d Henry has a tablet that is 12 inches long. Lucas has a phone that is 6 inches long. How long are the tablet and phone together?

_____ _____ _____ = _____ inches

e Ella has a necklace that is 12 inches long. Nora has a necklace that is 10 inches long. How much longer is Ella's necklace?

_____ _____ _____ = _____ inches

f Kiki ran 50 feet. Lily ran 43 feet. How much farther did Kiki go?

_____ _____ _____ = _____ feet

g Sam chased his friend at recess. First, he ran 26 feet. Then, he ran 32 feet. How far did he run in all?

_____ _____ _____ = _____ feet

TIME AND MONEY

Digital Clocks

Digital clocks use numbers to show the time.

The numbers on this side show the hours. The hour is 7.  The numbers on this side show the minutes. The minutes are 25.

The time is 7:25.

Example 1: What time does each clock show?

a  4:15

b  6:10

c  8:30

d  2:00

The numbers on a digital clock may look different than the numbers you write.

Your turn

1. Match the times on the clocks to the words.

● 3:15 — three forty

a 7:35 — seven thirty-five

b 11:20 — three fifteen

c  — eleven twenty

SELF CHECK Mark how you feel

Got it!   Need help...   I don't get it

Check your answers
How many did you get correct?

TIME AND MONEY — Practice

1 Write each time in words.

- 4:00 — four o'clock
- a 6:15 — _____
- b 11:40 — _____
- c 5:55 — _____
- d 3:10 — _____
- e 7:20 — _____

2 Write the times on the digital clocks.

- twelve fifteen — 12:15
- a eight twenty — ☐
- b three o'clock — ☐
- c four thirty — ☐
- d twelve fifteen — ☐
- e nine forty — ☐

3 Match the times on the clocks to the words.

- 2:00 → two o'clock
- a 2:40
- b 12:40
- c 6:00
- d 10:15
- e 1:10

twelve forty
six o'clock
ten fifteen
two o'clock
one ten
two forty

TIME AND MONEY

Analog Clocks: 00 and 30

An analog clock has moving hands that show the time. The numbers 1 through 12 tell you the time.

An analog clock has two hands. The short one is the hour hand. The long one is the minute hand.

SCAN to watch video

Example 1: This clock shows 2:00, or two o'clock.

The minute hand is pointing at the 12. The hour has just begun.

The hour hand is pointing at the 2.

Example 2: This clock shows 5:30, or five thirty. The hour hand is between the 5 and 6. It is halfway between 5 o'clock and 6 o'clock.

Each small line around the clock is 1 minute.

The minute hand is pointing to the 6. That means it is 30 minutes past the hour.

Write the hour first, then the minutes. The time on the clock is 5:30.

Your turn

① What time is on each clock?

6:00

The hour hand moves around the clock slowly. The minute hand moves around the clock each hour.

a  _____

SELF CHECK   Mark how you feel

Check your answers
How many did you get correct?

TIME AND MONEY

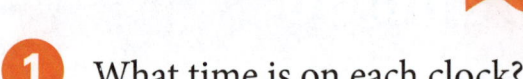

1 What time is on each clock?

  11:30

c  _____

a  _____

d  _____

b  _____

e  _____

2 Draw the times on the clocks.

  5:00

c  9:00

a  7:00

d  2:30

b  5:30

e  10:30

Analog Clocks: 15 and 45

Imagine the clock is cut into four equal parts, or quarters. Each quarter is 15 minutes. All together, the four quarters equal 60 minutes, or an hour.

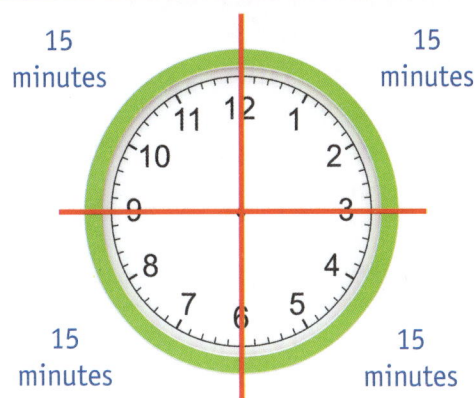

Example 1: The minute hand points to the 3. This means it is 15 minutes past the hour. The time is **5:15**.

Example 2: The hour hand is between the 8 and 9. This means it is between the 8th and 9th hours. The minute hand points to the 9. This means it is 45 minutes past the hour. The time is **8:45**.

Your turn

1 What is the time on each clock?

• _7:15_

b _____

a _____

c _____

Some people read these times as "quarter to" or "quarter past."

SELF CHECK Mark how you feel
- Got it!
- Need help...
- I don't get it

Check your answers How many did you get correct?

TIME AND MONEY

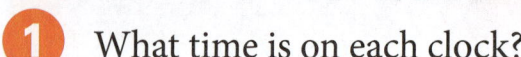

1 What time is on each clock?

  **5:45**

c  _____

a  _____

d  _____

b  _____

e  _____

2 Draw the times on the clocks.

  3:45

c  7:45

a  5:45

d  11:45

b  9:15

e  11:15

210 146444—Catch-Up Math © Shell Education

TIME AND MONEY

Five-Minute Intervals

Each number on the clock is a 5-minute jump in time. This is called an interval.

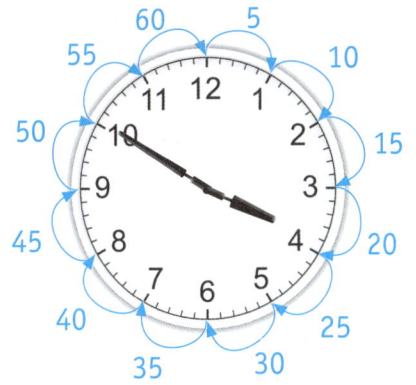

There are 60 minutes in 1 hour.

Each jump is 5 minutes. The black numbers show which hour it is. The blue numbers show the minutes.

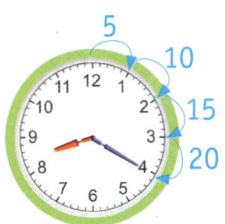      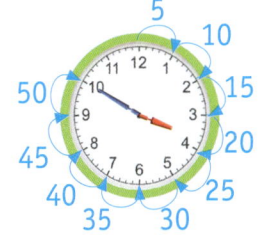

Example 1: The small hand is on the 8. The big hand is on the 4. Count 5-minute intervals from 12. The time is **8:20**.

Example 2: The small hand is between the 10 and 11. The big hand is on the 7. Count 5-minute intervals from 12. The time is **10:35**.

Example 3: The small hand is between the 3 and 4. The big hand is on the 10. The time is **3:50**.

 Write the time. Draw the jumps if you need to.

•  7:25   a  _____

SELF CHECK   Mark how you feel

 Got it!    Need help...    I don't get it

Check your answers

How many did you get correct?

TIME AND MONEY

Practice

1 Write the time shown on each clock.

 **3:20**

 c _____

 a _____

 d _____

 b _____

 e _____

2 Match the times on the clocks.

 a

 b

 c

 d

3:50

6:20

5:35

10:35

2:10

TIME AND MONEY

Elapsed Time

You can solve word problems about elapsed time. Elapsed time tells how much time has passed.

Example 1: Ben leaves his house at 8:00 for school. He arrives at school at 8:30. How long does it take him to get to school?

You can use a number line to solve the problem. Count up by 10s to see how many minutes have passed. It took him **30 minutes** to get to school.

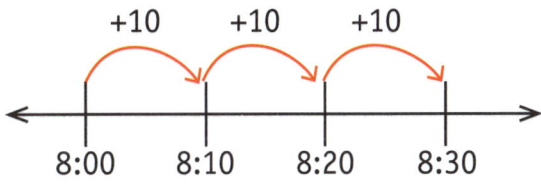

Example 2: Aiden starts a movie at 6:00. It finishes at 8:00. How long was the movie?

Count by hours to see how much time has passed. The movie was **2 hours** long.

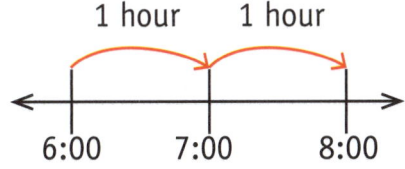

Your turn

1 Solve each word problem. Use the number line to help you.

● Mara practices piano after school. She starts at 4:00. She ends at 4:30. How long does she practice?

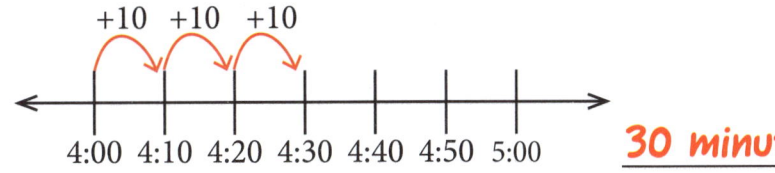

30 minutes

Solve elapsed time problems by counting from the start time to the end time.

a Becca starts to eat dinner at 6:00. She finishes at 6:30. How long does Becca eat?

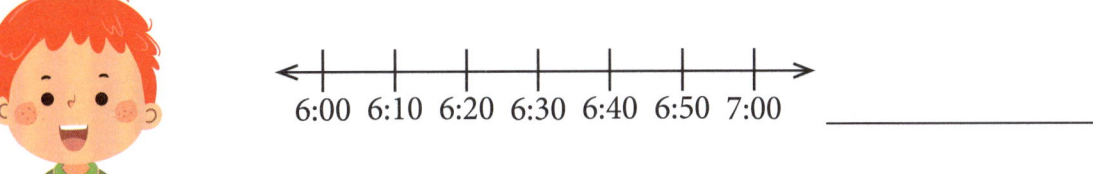

SELF CHECK — Mark how you feel
Got it! | Need help... | I don't get it

Check your answers — How many did you get correct?

TIME AND MONEY

Practice

1 Solve each word problem. Use the number line to help you.

Annie does her chores. Her mom says she has to work for 30 minutes. If she starts at 4:00, what time does she finish?

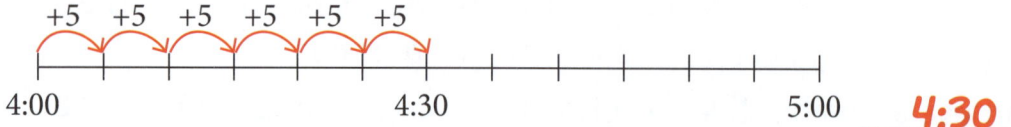

4:30

a James goes to the arcade at 1:00. His mom says he has 30 minutes to play there. When does he have to leave?

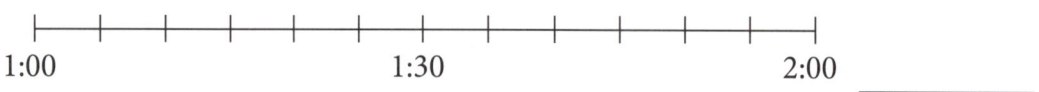

b Hector has 30 minutes until his mom picks him up. It is 5:30. What time will his mom come?

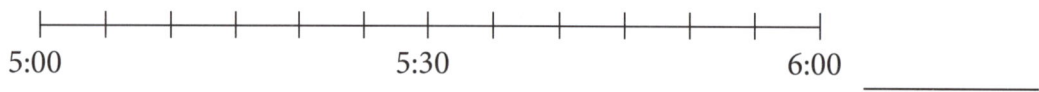

c Jackson cannot wait for school to end at 3:00. It is 2:00 right now. How long does he have to wait?

d Avery has homework to do for 30 minutes. She wants to start at 5:00. What time will she be done?

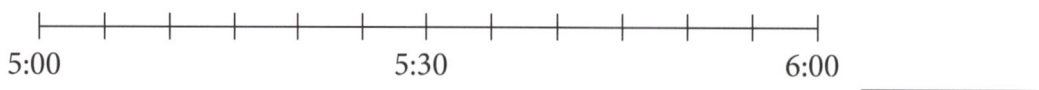

e Sofia is running late. The party starts at 2:30. Her map says she will not arrive until 3:00. How many minutes is she late?

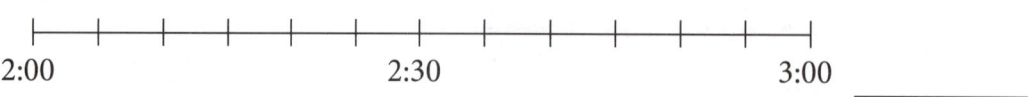

TIME AND MONEY

Adding Coins

Coins and bills have different values.

These are the values of each coin.

A penny is worth one cent, 1¢.

A nickel is worth five cents, 5¢.

A dime is worth ten cents, 10¢.

A quarter is worth twenty-five cents, 25¢.

There is also a dollar coin, but it is not used often.

A dollar bill is worth one dollar, $1.00. A dollar is the same as 100¢.

Example 1: How much money is there?

This is for the one dollar.

There is one dollar and 37 cents. This is written $1.37.

This is for the 37 cents.

Your turn

1 Write how much money is in each set.

    _____35¢_____

a   _____

b     _____

SELF CHECK Mark how you feel

Got it!  Need help...  I don't get it

Check your answers How many did you get correct?

TIME AND MONEY

Practice

1 Write how much money is in each set.

      **25¢**

a   _____

b    _____

c        _____

d   _____

e     _____

f    _____

g    _____

h       _____

i
     _____

TIME AND MONEY

Money Word Problems

You can solve word problems about money. Read the problems carefully. Look for clues to know if you need to add or subtract.

Example 1: Missy has a quarter. Marcus has a dime and a nickel. How much more money does Missy have?

 Missy
25¢

 Marcus
15¢

25¢ − 15¢ = **10¢**

Example 2: Small candies cost 12¢ each. How much would 2 candies cost?

12¢ + 12¢ = **24¢**

Example 3: Jessie has $1.00. She buys a sticker for 50¢. How much change does she get back?

100¢ − 50¢ = **50¢**

Remember that a dollar is worth 100 cents!

 Your turn

1. Write an equation to solve each word problem.

   • Mira has 30¢ in her piggy bank. She adds 2 dimes. How much does she have now?

   __30¢__ + __20¢__ = __50¢__

   a   Daniel needs 50¢ for a toy. He has 15¢ already. How much more does he need?

   _____ − _____ = _____

   b   Haley has two nickels. Her sister has two dimes. How much do they have all together?

   _____ + _____ = _____

SELF CHECK Mark how you feel

Got it! ☐   Need help... ☐   I don't get it ☐

Check your answers
How many did you get correct?

TIME AND MONEY

Practice

1 Write equations to solve the word problems.

Jane was looking for coins. She found a quarter on Monday. On Tuesday, she found 3 dimes. How much did she find in all?

   _25¢_ + _30¢_ = _55¢_

a Mom gave Riley 52¢. Dad gave Riley 42¢. How much does Riley have now?

   _____ + _____ = _____

b Monica had 80¢. She spent 30¢. How much does she have now?

   _____ − _____ = _____

c Sofia has 4 quarters. She wants to have $3.00. How much more money does she need?

   _____ − _____ = _____

d Eli has 2 dimes, 2 nickels, and 3 pennies. He wants a small toy that costs 25¢. Does he have enough? Explain.

   _____ + _____ + _____ = _____

   _____

e Hank has 3 quarters and 2 pennies. Paula has 2 quarters and 3 dimes. Who has more money?

   Hank: _____ + _____ = _____

   Paula: _____ + _____ = _____

   _____ has more money.

f Iris has 1 dollar, 2 quarters, 3 dimes and 5 pennies. How much money does she have all together?

   _____ + _____ + _____ + _____ = _____

Time and Money Review

1 Write the time shown on each clock.

a  d

_____ _____

b  e

_____ _____

c  f

_____ _____

2 Draw the times on the clocks.

a 8:00 d 11:45

b 1:30 e 12:10

c 5:15 f 3:35

TIME AND MONEY

Review

3 Match the clocks to the correct times.

a    3:00

b    2:15

c    11:30

d    6:00

e    12:40

f    10:10

4 Write the time shown on each digital clock.

a  _____ d  _____

b  _____ e  _____

c  _____ f  _____

Review

TIME AND MONEY

5 Write how much money is in each set.

a. 3 dimes + 4 pennies = _____

b. 1 dime + 3 nickels = _____

c. 1 dime + 4 nickels + 4 pennies = _____

d. 1 dime + 4 nickels = _____

e. 3 dimes + 3 nickels = _____

f. 1 quarter + 3 dimes + 3 nickels = _____

g. 1 quarter + 2 dimes + 4 pennies = _____

h. $1 + 3 nickels + 2 pennies = _____

i. $1 + 2 quarters + 1 nickel = _____

j. $1 + 2 dimes + 1 nickel + 2 nickels + 2 pennies = _____

TIME AND MONEY

Review

6 Solve each problem about elapsed time. Use the number line to help you.

a Roberto gets out of school at 2:30. He walks home for 30 minutes. What time does he get home?

2:00   2:30   3:00   _____

b Piper needs to be at her tennis game at 5:00. It takes 30 minutes to drive there. What time should she leave?

4:00   4:30   5:00   _____

7 Solve each word problem about money.

a Gum costs 27¢. Candy costs 51¢. How much do they cost all together?

_____ + _____ = _____

b Heather had 3 quarters. She spent 1 quarter. How much does she have now?

_____ − _____ = _____

c Stan has $4.00. He wants to have $20.00. How much more money does he need?

_____ − _____ = _____

d Ava has 4 dimes, 2 nickels, and 4 pennies. How much money does she have all together?

_____ + _____ + _____ = _____

Answers

1. WHOLE NUMBERS

Read and Write Whole Numbers

Page 9 — Your Turn

1. a forty-six
   b 220
   c eighty-eight
   d 73

Page 10 — Practice

1. a 92
   b 65
   c 23
   d 12
   e 99
   f 59
   g 134
   h 272
   i 340
   j 107
   k 511

2. a thirty-one
   b eighty-seven
   c twenty-five
   d fifty-five
   e sixty
   f one hundred forty-three
   g two hundred fifteen
   h three hundred seventy-eight
   i two hundred one
   j four hundred fifty

Count by Tens

Page 11 — Your Turn

1. a 50; 70
   b 11; 51

Page 12 — Practice

1. a 40; 60
   b 20; 30; 50; 60
   c 30; 40; 50
   d 60; 70; 80
   e 50; 60; 70; 80

2. a 60; 50; 20
   b 70; 60
   c 30; 20; 10
   d 70; 50; 30
   e 50; 40; 30; 20

3.

1	2	3	4	5	6	7	8	9	10
11	12	13	14	15	16	17	18	19	20
21	22	23	24	25	26	27	28	29	30
31	32	33	34	35	36	37	38	39	40
41	42	43	44	45	46	47	48	49	50
51	52	53	54	55	56	57	58	59	60
61	62	63	64	65	66	67	68	69	70
71	72	73	74	75	76	77	78	79	80
81	82	83	84	85	86	87	88	89	90
91	92	93	94	95	96	97	98	99	100

Count by Fives

Page 13 — Your Turn

1. a 10; 15
   b 60; 70
   c 80; 75; 70
   d 60; 50; 45

Page 14 — Practice

1. a 15; 20
   b 30; 40; 50
   c 60; 50; 40
   d 20; 25; 30; 35
   e 15; 20; 25; 30
   f 55; 60; 65; 70
   g 85; 80; 75; 70
   h 35; 30; 25; 20

2.

1	2	3	4	5	6	7	8	9	10
11	12	13	14	15	16	17	18	19	20
21	22	23	24	25	26	27	28	29	30
31	32	33	34	35	36	37	38	39	40
41	42	43	44	45	46	47	48	49	50
51	52	53	54	55	56	57	58	59	60
61	62	63	64	65	66	67	68	69	70
71	72	73	74	75	76	77	78	79	80
81	82	83	84	85	86	87	88	89	90
91	92	93	94	95	96	97	98	99	100

Count by Twenty-Fives

Page 15 — Your Turn

1. a 250; 275; 300
   b 525; 550
   c 775; 800
   d 625; 650; 675

Answers

Page 16 — Practice

1.

Count by Hundreds

Page 17 — Your Turn

1. a 400; 500; 700   c 500; 400; 300
   b 200; 400; 500   d 700; 600; 500

Page 18 — Practice

1. a 400   d 200   g 842
   b 700   e 500
   c 300   f 925

2. a 300   d 0   g 110
   b 200   e 400
   c 600   f 706

3. a 700; 500; 400; 300   c 222; 322; 422; 622
   b 500; 600; 700; 900   d 600; 700; 800; 900

Odd and Even Numbers

Page 19 — Your Turn

1. a even   c odd   e even
   b even   d odd

Page 20 — Practice

1. a 5 is odd.   b 12 is even.   c 7 is odd.

2. a 22, 24, 26, 28
   b 51, 53, 55, 57, 59
   c 46, 48, 50, 52

3.

1	2	3	4	5	6	7	8	9	10
11	12	13	14	15	16	17	18	19	20
21	22	23	24	25	26	27	28	29	30

(Even numbers circled: 2, 4, 6, 8, 10, 12, 14, 16, 18, 20, 22, 24, 26, 28, 30)

Add Odd and Even Numbers

Page 21 — Your Turn

1. a 4   c 14   e 8
   b 20   d 18   f 26

Page 22 — Practice

1. a 22   c 40   e 16   g 30
   b 8   d 12   f 10

2. (Circled: 3 + 4; 7 + 29; 2 + 22; 19 + 19; 26 + 45; 78 + 66; 31 + 101)
   (Not circled: 11 + 14)

3. Check that sums are even. Possible answers:
   a 9 + 9 = 18   b 13 + 3 = 16   c 24 + 10 = 34

4. Check that sums are odd. Possible answers:
   a 7 + 10 = 17   b 12 + 9 = 21   c 11 + 8 = 19

One-Step Word Problems

Page 23 — Your Turn

1. a 18 − 10 = 8 stickers

Page 24 — Practice

1. a 8 + 4 = 12 candles
   b 14 − 7 = 7 soccer balls
   c 3 + 4 = 7 pizza slices
   d 4 + 7 = 11 marbles
   e 10 − 3 = 7 dogs
   f 12 − 3 = 9 coins

2. a 8 + 5 = 13 paintbrushes
   b 4 + 7 = 11 petals
   c 14 − 6 = 8 airplanes
   d 9 − 5 = 4 monkeys
   e 3 + 5 = 8 berries
   f 7 + 7 = 14 cards

Answers

Two-Step Word Problems

Page 26 — Your Turn

1. a **Step 1:** 12 – 2 = 10   **Step 2:** 10 – 4 = 6
      Answer: There were 6 balls left.

Page 27 — Practice

1. a **Step 1:** 4 + 4 = 8   **Step 2:** 8 + 5 = 13
      Answer: James saw 13 birds in all.
   b **Step 1:** 5 + 2 = 7   **Step 2:** 7 + 6 = 13
      Answer: There were 13 helpers in all.
   c **Step 1:** 4 + 3 = 7   **Step 2:** 7 + 6 = 13
      Answer: The dog had 13 treats in all.
   d **Step 1:** 10 + 3 = 13   **Step 2:** 13 + 3 = 16
      Answer: She read 16 pages in all.
2. a **Step 1:** 15 – 4 = 11   **Step 2:** 11 – 6 = 5
      Answer: There were 5 pairs left.
   b **Step 1:** 16 – 4 = 12   **Step 2:** 12 – 5 = 7
      Answer: 7 kids walked home.
   c **Step 1:** 10 – 2 = 8   **Step 2:** 8 – 3 = 5
      Answer: 5 kids wore pants.
   d **Step 1:** 15 – 10 = 5   **Step 2:** 5 – 3 = 2
      Answer: Danny had 2 animal toys.
3. a **Step 1:** 10 + 4 = 14   **Step 2:** 14 – 2 = 12
      Answer: There were 12 papers left.
   b **Step 1:** 11 + 5 = 16   **Step 2:** 16 – 3 = 13
      Answer: There were 13 coins left.
   c **Step 1:** 5 + 4 = 9   **Step 2:** 9 – 2 = 7
      Answer: There were 7 paintings left.
   d **Step 1:** 14 + 3 = 17   **Step 2:** 17 – 6 = 11
      Answer: There were 11 blocks left.

Expanded Form

Page 30 — Your Turn

1. a 369 = 300 + 60 + 9   c 712 = 700 + 10 + 2
   b 453 = 400 + 50 + 3
2. a 40   b 7   c 300

Page 31 — Practice

1. a 3 hundreds + 1 ten + 2 ones
   b 4 hundreds + 7 tens + 5 ones
   c 1 hundred + 0 tens + 8 ones
2. a 432   b 261   c 187   d 256
3. a 5   c 60   e 7
   b 400   d 30
4. a ⓼90, 680, ⓼12, 348, 788
   b 2⓺, 761, 84⓺, 165, 96⓺
   c ⓻6, 47, ⓶75, 763, 2⓻⓻
5. a 426 = 400 + 20 + 6   f 350 = 300 + 50
   b 835 = 800 + 30 + 5   g 961 = 900 + 60 + 1
   c 180 = 100 + 80   h 718 = 700 + 10 + 8
   d 592 = 500 + 90 + 2   i 219 = 200 + 10 + 9
   e 844 = 800 + 40 + 4

Order Numbers

Page 33 — Your Turn

1. a 12, 53, 76   b 118, 144, 262
2. a 973, 458, 210   b 323, 232, 133

Page 34 — Practice

1. a 18, 81, 89
   b 24, 45, 52
   c 76, 91, 97
   d 110, 235, 303
   e 95, 105, 204, 244, 501
   f 294, 487, 566, 578, 655
   g 176, 184, 193, 195, 299
2. a 56, 37, 27
   b 77, 65, 33
   c 68, 36, 29
   d 323, 232, 133
   e 800, 782, 600, 599, 400
   f 825, 785, 685, 681, 485
   g 601, 570, 513, 509, 489

Answers

Whole Numbers Review—Page 35

1.

	Base-Ten Blocks	Standard Form	Words
a		26	twenty-six
b		35	thirty-five
c		62	sixty-two
d		41	forty-one
e		55	fifty-five
f		13	thirteen

2. a 300; 500; 600
   d 100; 125; 150
   b 6; 8
   e 45; 50
   c 50; 70

3. a 65, 68, 75, 78, 88
   b 291, 511, 596, 750, 754
   c 32, 45, 99, 113, 139

4. a 511, 322, 257, 115, 97
   b 677, 588, 578, 478, 294
   c 399, 195, 193, 178, 167

5. a She has 16 stuffed animals.
   b He had 7 markers left.

6. a 387 = 300 + 80 + 7
   b 435 = 400 + 30 + 5
   c 673 = 600 + 70 + 3
   d 875 = 800 + 70 + 5
   e 112 = 100 + 10 + 2

7. a 641   c 457   e 473
   b 268   d 593   f 205

8. a 187 = one hundred eighty-seven
   b 935 = nine hundred thirty-five
   c 712 = seven hundred twelve
   d 254 = two hundred fifty-four
   e 356 = three hundred fifty-six

2. MENTAL MATH

Fact Families to 20

Page 38 — Your Turn

1. a 3 + 5 = 8   8 − 5 = 3
      5 + 3 = 8   8 − 3 = 5

Page 39 — Practice

1. a 6 + 8 = 14   d 7 + 6 = 13
      8 + 6 = 14   6 + 7 = 13
      14 − 6 = 8   13 − 7 = 6
      14 − 8 = 6   13 − 6 = 7
   b 8 + 2 = 10   e 8 + 3 = 11
      2 + 8 = 10   3 + 8 = 11
      10 − 2 = 8   11 − 3 = 8
      10 − 8 = 2   11 − 8 = 3
   c 7 + 4 = 11
      4 + 7 = 11
      11 − 4 = 7
      11 − 7 = 4

2. a 5 + 7 = 12   d 3 + 7 = 10
      7 + 5 = 12   7 + 3 = 10
      12 − 7 = 5   10 − 7 = 3
      12 − 5 = 7   10 − 3 = 7
   b 3 + 8 = 11   e 4 + 6 = 10
      8 + 3 = 11   6 + 4 = 10
      11 − 8 = 3   10 − 6 = 4
      11 − 3 = 8   10 − 4 = 6
   c 2 + 6 = 8
      6 + 2 = 8
      8 − 6 = 2
      8 − 2 = 6

Answers

Count On

Page 40 — Your Turn

1. a 5 + 7 = 12
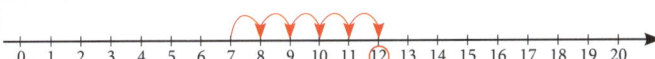

Page 41 — Practice

1. a 9 + 4 = 13

   b 7 + 2 = 9

   c 6 + 8 = 14
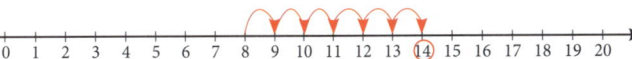

   d 9 + 2 = 11
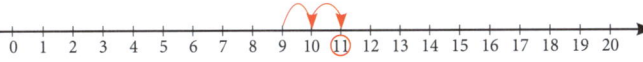

   e 5 + 13 = 18
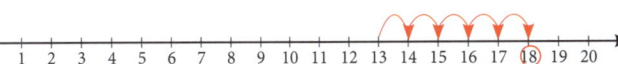

   f 15 + 4 = 19
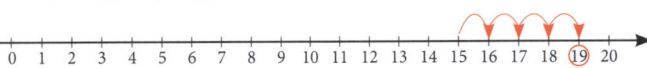

   g 3 + 17 = 20
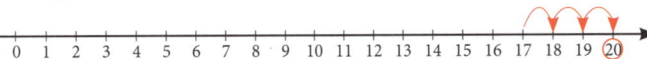

2. a 10   d 15   g 13
   b 9   e 13
   c 13   f 13

3. a 19   d 17   g 26
   b 25   e 21
   c 28   f 26

4. a 14   d 29   g 27
   b 14   e 23
   c 10   f 24

Count Back

Page 43 — Your Turn

1. a 7 − 4 = 3
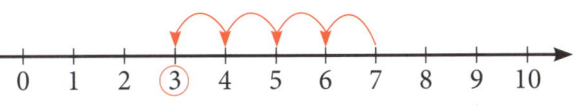

Page 44 — Practice

1. a 13 − 4 = 9
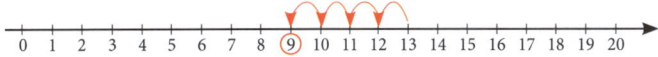

   b 9 − 2 = 7
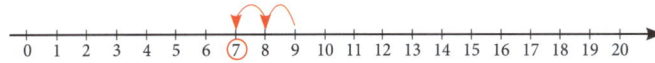

   c 15 − 6 = 9
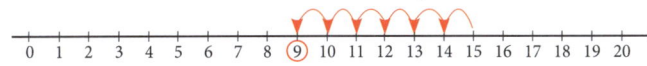

   d 17 − 5 = 12
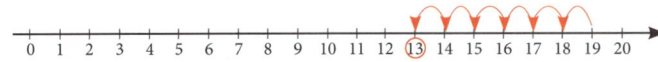

   e 19 − 6 = 13
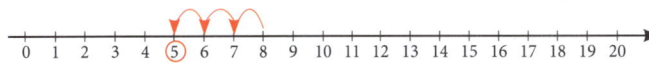

   f 8 − 3 = 5
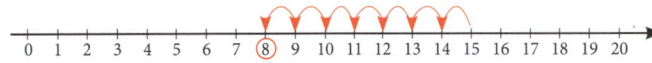

   g 15 − 7 = 8

Make Tens

Page 45 — Your Turn

1. a 7 + 5 = 12   b 8 + 3 = 11
      [3][2]   [2][1]

Page 46 — Practice

1. a 9 + 1 = 10   f 4 + 6 = 10
   b 8 + 2 = 10   g 3 + 7 = 10
   c 7 + 3 = 10   h 2 + 8 = 10
   d 6 + 4 = 10   i 1 + 9 = 10
   e 5 + 5 = 10

3. a 5 + 5 = 10   e 3 + 7 = 10
   b 6 + 4 = 10   f 0 + 10 = 10
   c 1 + 9 = 10   g 8 + 2 = 10
   d 8 + 2 = 10

© Shell Education   146444—Catch-Up Math   227

Answers

4. a 7 + 4 = 11
      3 1
   b 8 + 5 = 13
      2 3
   c 6 + 9 = 15
      4 5
   d 6 + 6 = 12
      4 2
   e 9 + 8 = 17
      1 7

   f 6 + 7 = 13
      4 3
   g 7 + 5 = 12
      3 2
   h 9 + 5 = 14
      1 4
   i 8 + 8 = 16
      2 6

Doubles + or − 1

Page 48 — Your Turn
1. a 9   b 15   c 17

Page 49 — Practice
1. a 2   d 4   g 8
   b 6   e 22   h 12
   c 16   f 14   i 20

2. a 5 + 5 = 10
      5 + 5 + 1 = 11
      5 + 5 − 1 = 9
   b 3 + 3 = 6
      3 + 3 + 1 = 7
      3 + 3 − 1 = 5
   c 8 + 8 = 16
      8 + 8 + 1 = 17
      8 + 8 − 1 = 15
   d 2 + 2 = 4
      2 + 2 + 1 = 5
      2 + 2 − 1 = 3
   e 11 + 11 = 22
      11 + 11 + 1 = 23
      11 + 11 − 1 = 21

Commutative Property

Page 50 — Your Turn
1. a 4 + 8 = 12   8 + 4 = 12
   b 8 + 5 = 13   5 + 8 = 13
   c 5 + 9 = 14   9 + 5 = 14
   d 6 + 7 = 13   7 + 6 = 13

Page 51 — Practice
1. a 3 + 8 = 11   8 + 3 = 11
   b 4 + 6 = 10   6 + 4 = 10
   c 5 + 4 = 9   4 + 5 = 9
   d 7 + 5 = 12   5 + 7 = 12
   e 8 + 6 = 14   6 + 8 = 14
2. a 6 + 4 + 2 = 12   2 + 6 + 4 = 12
   b 4 + 5 + 3 = 12   5 + 3 + 4 = 12
   c 6 + 4 + 5 = 15   4 + 5 + 6 = 15
   d 6 + 7 + 3 = 16   3 + 6 + 7 = 16
   e 3 + 8 + 2 = 13   8 + 3 + 2 = 13
3. Equations should use the same numbers and be true equations.

Addition Facts to 20

Page 52 — Your Turn
1. a 8   e 12   i 8
   b 6   f 12   j 8
   c 6   g 11
   d 8   h 9

Page 53 — Practice
1.

+	1	2	3	4	5	6	7	8	9	10
1	2	3	4	5	6	7	8	9	10	11
2	3	4	5	6	7	8	9	10	11	12
3	4	5	6	7	8	9	10	11	12	13
4	5	6	7	8	9	10	11	12	13	14
5	6	7	8	9	10	11	12	13	14	15
6	7	8	9	10	11	12	13	14	15	16
7	8	9	10	11	12	13	14	15	16	17
8	9	10	11	12	13	14	15	16	17	18
9	10	11	12	13	14	15	16	17	18	19
10	11	12	13	14	15	16	17	18	19	20

3. a 6   g 10   m 3   s 15
   b 9   h 10   n 10   t 12
   c 8   i 10   o 10   u 17
   d 8   j 5   p 3
   e 6   k 7   q 7
   f 11   l 14   r 9

Answers

Subtraction Facts to 20

Page 55 — Your Turn

1. a 2 e 8 i 2
    b 4 f 10 j 2
    c 5 g 9
    d 7 h 6

Page 56 — Practice

1. a 3   g 11   m 1   s 9
    b 10 h 6   n 15 t 8
    c 6   i 4   o 4   u 9
    d 7   j 10   p 3
    e 4   k 7   q 6
    f 9   l 5   r 8

Mental Math Review—Page 57

1. a 5 + 8 = 13   c 8 + 6 = 14
       8 + 5 = 13   6 + 8 = 14
       13 − 5 = 8   14 − 8 = 6
       13 − 8 = 5   14 − 6 = 8
    b 3 + 6 = 9   d 5 + 10 = 15
       6 + 3 = 9   10 + 5 = 15
       9 − 6 = 3   15 − 5 = 10
       9 − 3 = 6   15 − 10 = 5

2. a 9 + 6 = 15   c 1 + 9 = 10
       6 + 9 = 15   9 + 1 = 10
       15 − 9 = 6   10 − 1 = 9
       15 − 6 = 9   10 − 9 = 1
    b 5 + 3 = 8   d 5 + 9 = 14
       3 + 5 = 8   9 + 5 = 14
       8 − 3 = 5   14 − 5 = 9
       8 − 5 = 3   14 − 9 = 5

3. a 8 + 3 = 11   d 7 + 8 = 15
          [2][1]   [5][2]
    b 9 + 5 = 14   e 9 + 9 = 18
          [1][4]   [1][8]
    c 6 + 8 = 14   f 7 + 7 = 14
          [4][2]   [3][4]

4. a 5 + 6 = 11
    b 7 + 3 = 10
    c 5 + 7 = 12   7 + 5 = 12
    d 3 + 6 = 9   6 + 3 = 9
    e 9 + 3 = 12   3 + 9 = 12
    f 6 + 8 = 14   8 + 6 = 14

5. a 2 + 3 + 4 = 9
    b 3 + 6 + 5 = 14
    c 5 + 4 + 6 = 15   5 + 6 + 4 = 15
    d 7 + 8 + 5 = 20   5 + 7 + 8 = 20
    e 8 + 7 + 3 = 18   3 + 8 + 7 = 18
    f 2 + 8 + 9 = 19   9 + 8 + 2 = 19

6. Check that numbers add to the correct sums.

7. a 9   i 10
    b 8   j 6
    c 12   k 8
    d 18   l 13
    e 14   m 20
    f 6   n 17
    g 17   o 16
    h 15

8. a 3   f 7   k 6
    b 2   g 4   l 6
    c 16   h 5   m 10
    d 11   i 9   n 7
    e 10   j 1   o 12

3. PLACE VALUE

Tens and Ones

Page 61 — Your Turn

1. a 4 tens 6 ones
    b 5 tens 2 ones
    c 1 ten 7 ones
    d 9 tens 3 ones

Answers

Page 62 — Practice

1.

	Number	Tens	Ones
a	41		
b	72		
c	58		
d	30		
e	17		
f	67		
g	81		

2. a 63 = 6 tens 3 ones
      63 = 60 + 3

   b 37 = 3 tens 7 ones
      37 = 30 + 7

   c 81 = 8 tens 1 one
      81 = 80 + 1

   d 16 = 1 ten 6 ones
      16 = 10 + 6

   e 25 = 2 tens 5 ones
      25 = 20 + 5

   f 72 = 7 tens 2 ones
      72 = 70 + 2

Greater Than, Less Than, Equal To

Page 64 — Your Turn

1. a True   c True   e True
   b False   d False

Page 65 — Practice

1. a equal to   e equal to
   b less than   f less than
   c greater than   g greater than
   d less than

2. a <   c <   e >   g =
   b =   d <   f <

3. a 44, 49, 5   d 60, 6
   b 37   e 81, 85
   c 54, 57

4. a Accept any number 41–59.
   b Accept any number 21–79.
   c Accept any number 37–85.
   d Accept any number 23–25.
   e Accept any number 79–87.
   f Accept any number 40–49.
   g Accept 53 or 54.
   h Accept any number 51–59.
   i Accept any number 12–21.
   j Accept any number 40–48.
   k Accept any number 41–43.
   l Accept any number 79–81.
   m Accept any number 21–24.
   n Accept any number 7–14.
   o Accept any number 58–66.
   p Accept any number 33–41.
   q Accept any number 41–43.
   r Accept any number 46–61.
   s Accept any number 88–98.

5. Accept any two numbers that correctly complete each comparison.

Compare Three-Digit Numbers

Page 67 — Your Turn

1. a greater than
   b less than
   c equal to
   d less than

Page 68 — Practice

1. a True   e False
   b False   f True
   c True   g False
   d True

230 146444—Catch-Up Math   © Shell Education

Answers

2. a 200, 215
    b 204, 200
    c 390, 400
    d 200, 201
    e 400
3. Accept any two numbers that correctly complete each comparison.
4. a less than   e less than
    b less than   f greater than
    c equal to   g greater than
    d greater than
5. a <   c =   e =   g <
    b >   d >   f <
6. a Accept any number 404–679.
    b Accept any number 197–379.
    c Accept any number 102–975.
    d Accept any number 112–184.
    e Accept any number 325–422.
    f Accept any number 980–984.
    g Accept any number 433–543.
    h 640
    i Accept any number 292–296.

10 More and 10 Less
Page 70 — Your Turn
1. a 86   b 34

Page 71 — Practice
1. a 42   d 97   g 32   j 56
    b 69   e 56   h 50   k 66
    c 24   f 89   i 46
2. Check that equations correctly add 10.
3. a 45   f 52   k 23
    b 87   g 40   l 46
    c 13   h 27   m 70
    d 35   i 83
    e 49   j 58
4. Check that equations correctly subtract 10.

100 More and 100 Less
Page 73 — Your Turn
1. a 619   b 585   c 665   d 244

Page 74 — Practice
1. a 400   d 500   g 900
    b 300   e 200
    c 700   f 600
2. a 200   d 0   g 600
    b 300   e 500
    c 100   f 800
3. a 200   c 300   e 800
    b 100   d 900   f 700
4. a 444   d 664   g 767
    b 378   e 312
    c 712   f 786
5. a 255   d 787   g 408
    b 347   e 562
    c 177   f 345
6. a 330   c 361   e 988
    b 209   d 387   f 625

Place Value Review—Page 76
1. a 6 tens 2 ones   c 1 ten 8 ones
       60 + 2 = 62   10 + 8 = 18
    b 5 tens 2 ones   d 4 tens 4 ones
       50 + 2 = 52   40 + 4 = 44
2. a is less than   e is less than
    b is greater than   f is less than
    c is greater than   g is less than
    d is equal to   h is less than
3. a <   c >   e <   g =
    b <   d =   f >   h <
4. a 44, 49
    b 29
    c 29, 30
    d 74

Answers

5. a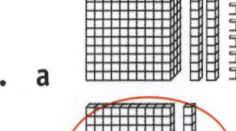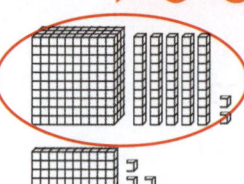

   b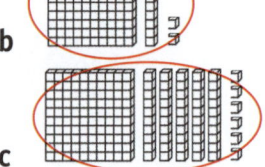

   c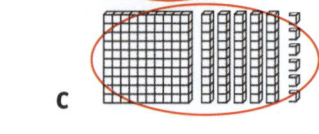

6. a 35   d 6   g 43
   b 77   e 86   h 30
   c 33   f 79   i 78

7. a 300   c 463
   b 200   d 865

8. a 700   c 300   e 700
   b 100   d 0   f 400

4. ADDITION

Add One- and Two-Digit Numbers

Page 79 — Your Turn

1. a 69   b 32   c 21

Page 80 — Practice

1. a 28   d 88   g 23
   b 39   e 60   h 40
   c 31   f 63   i 46

2. a 77   c 42   e 40
   b 98   d 32

3. a 60   d 70   g 35
   b 17   e 78   h 97
   c 49   f 84   i 66

4. a 65   c 95   e 90
   b 72   d 48

Use Base-Ten Blocks

Page 82 — Your Turn

1. a 45 + 24 = 69

Page 83 — Practice

1. a 25 + 3 = 28   c 12 + 11 = 23
   b 46 + 22 = 68

2. a 24 + 15 = 39   d 32 + 20 = 52

   b 31 + 47 = 78   e 23 + 12 = 35

   c 40 + 15 = 55

3. a 226 + 112 = 338   b 321 + 124 = 445

4. a 130 + 42 = 172
   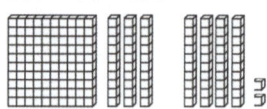

   b 110 + 17 = 127
   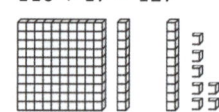

   c 235 + 20 = 255
   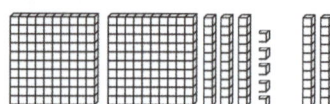

   d 127 + 31 = 158

   e 215 + 12 = 227
   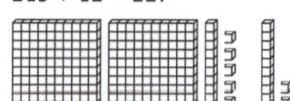

Addition with Number Lines

Page 85 — Your Turn

1. a 34 + 21 = 55
   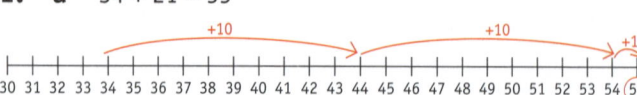

Answers

Page 86 — Practice

1. **a**   11 + 6 = 17

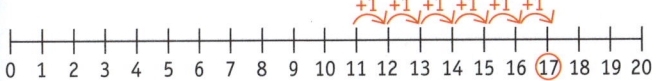

    b   18 + 5 = 23

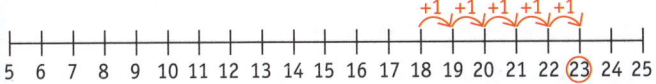

    c   14 + 8 = 22

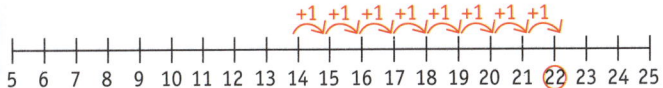

    d   17 + 4 = 21

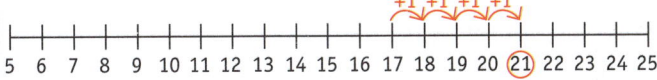

    e   21 + 7 = 28

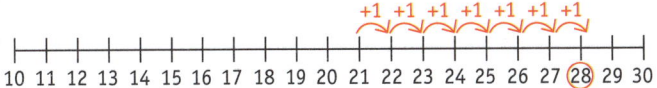

    f   12 + 9 = 21

2. **a**   25 + 16 = 41

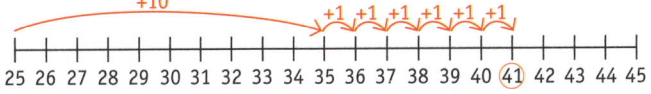

    b   34 + 16 = 50

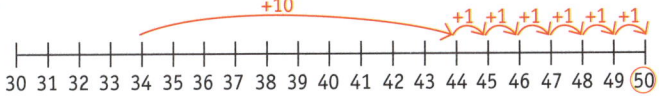

    c   20 + 18 = 38

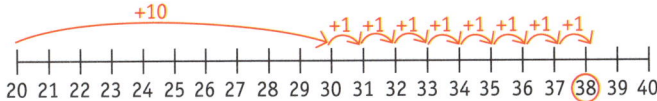

    d   32 + 24 = 56

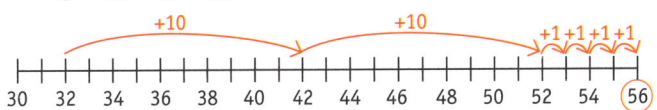

    e   64 + 21 = 85

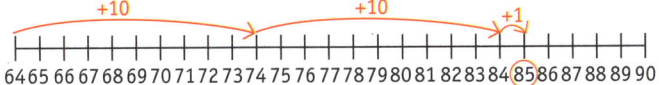

    f   38 + 15 = 53

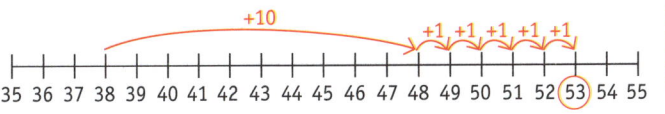

Add Tens and Ones

Page 88 — Your Turn

1. **a**   30 + 30 = 60   **b**   20 + 30 = 50

       5 + 5 = 10   2 + 6 = 8

       60 + 10 = 70   50 + 8 = 58

Page 89 — Practice

1. **a**   60 + 30 = 90   **c**   10 + 10 = 20

       9 + 2 = 11   8 + 8 = 16

       90 + 11 = 101   20 + 16 = 36

    b   20 + 10 = 30

       9 + 4 = 13

       30 + 13 = 43

2. **a**   30 + 50 = 80   **c**   10 + 70 = 80

       4 + 9 = 13   6 + 2 = 8

       80 + 13 = 93   80 + 8 = 88

    b   60 + 30 = 90

       2 + 3 = 5

       90 + 5 = 95

Unknown Addends

Page 90 — Your Turn

1. **a**   7 + 8 = 15

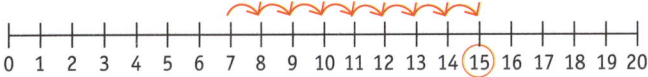

2. **a**   8 + 14 = 22   22 − 8 = 14

Page 91 — Practice

1. **a**   6 + 5 = 11

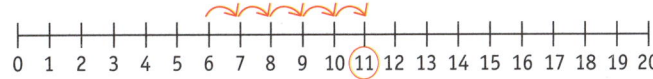

    b   5 + 7 = 12

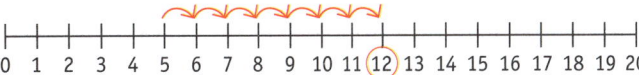

2. **a**   11 + 9 = 20   20 − 11 = 9

    b   26 + 10 = 36   36 − 26 = 10

    c   15 + 15 = 30   30 − 15 = 15

3. **a**   8 + 4 = 12   **d**   12 + 13 = 25

    b   15 + 8 = 23   **e**   10 + 18 = 28

    c   3 + 7 = 10

Answers

Add Three Numbers

Page 92 — Your Turn
1. a 14   b 16   c 13

Page 93 — Practice
1. a 18   d 11   g 18
   b 20   e 15   h 9
   c 16   f 16   i 10

2. a
   ```
     6
     4
   + 3
   ---
    13
   ```
   c
   ```
     4
     6
   + 3
   ---
    13
   ```
   e
   ```
     4
     6
   + 7
   ---
    17
   ```
   b
   ```
     8
     6
   + 2
   ---
    16
   ```
   d
   ```
     4
     3
   + 4
   ---
    11
   ```

Addition with Regrouping

Page 95 — Your Turn
1. a 65

Page 96 — Practice
1. a
   ```
     27
   + 25
   ----
     52
   ```
   c
   ```
     46
   + 46
   ----
     92
   ```
   e
   ```
     15
   + 19
   ----
     34
   ```
   b
   ```
     34
   + 29
   ----
     63
   ```
   d
   ```
     28
   + 35
   ----
     63
   ```

2. a 52   c 48   e 64
   b 51   d 40

Standard Addition Algorithm

Page 98 — Your Turn
1. a
   ```
     1
     34
   + 18
   ----
     52
   ```
   b
   ```
     1
     53
   + 29
   ----
     82
   ```

Page 99 — Practice
1. a
   ```
     1
     17
   + 17
   ----
     34
   ```
   d
   ```
     1
     28
   + 26
   ----
     54
   ```
   g
   ```
     1
     67
   + 14
   ----
     81
   ```
   b
   ```
     1
     54
   + 28
   ----
     82
   ```
   e
   ```
     1
     65
   + 27
   ----
     92
   ```
   h
   ```
     1
     29
   + 13
   ----
     42
   ```
   c
   ```
     1
     37
   + 25
   ----
     62
   ```
   f
   ```
     1
     19
   + 17
   ----
     36
   ```
   i
   ```
     1
     45
   + 27
   ----
     72
   ```

2. a 38   f 96
   b 76   g 73
   c 61   h 99
   d 66   i 73
   e 91   j 75

Add Three-Digit Numbers

Page 101 — Your Turn
1. a Hundreds: 100 + 100 = 200

   Tens: 50 + 40 = 90

   Ones: 6 + 8 = 14

   Total: 200 + 90 + 14 = 304

Page 102 — Practice
1. a 273   c 391   e 392
   b 393   d 535

2. a Hundreds: 200 + 200 = 400

   Tens: 10 + 20 = 30

   Ones: 4 + 8 = 12

   Total: 400 + 30 + 12 = 442

   b Hundreds: 300 + 100 = 400

   Tens: 10 + 60 = 70

   Ones: 5 + 6 = 11

   Total: 400 + 70 + 11 = 481

   c Hundreds: 200 + 100 = 300

   Tens: 10 + 40 = 50

   Ones: 8 + 5 = 13

   Total: 300 + 50 + 13 = 363

3. a 283   d 294
   b 362   e 341
   c 380

Addition Review—Page 104

1. a 31   e 58   i 67   m 27
   b 48   f 67   j 78   n 39
   c 35   g 45   k 68
   d 88   h 27   l 48

2. a 46 + 20 = 66   d 42 + 24 = 66
   b 52 + 32 = 84   e 32 + 26 = 58
   c 12 + 14 = 26

Answers

f   4 3
    + 1 1
      5 4

g   5 3
    + 2 2
      7 5

h   3 3
    + 1 1
      4 4

i   4 0
   + 2 2
     6 2

j   4 1
   + 1 8
     5 9

3. a   11 + 7 = 18

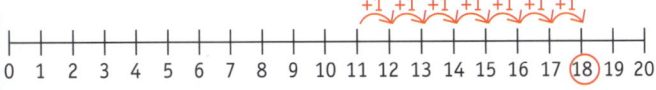

    b   12 + 4 = 16

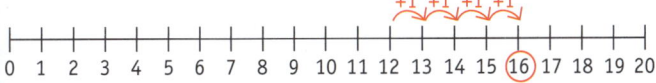

    c   19 + 3 = 22

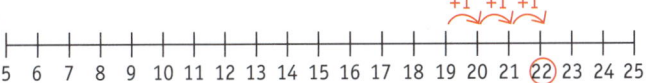

    d   20 + 3 = 23

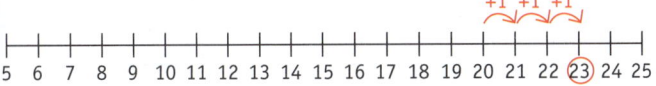

    e   15 + 7 = 22

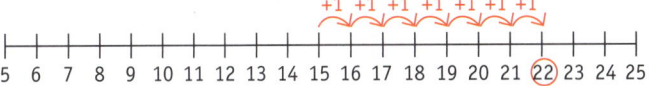

    f   35 + 18 = 53

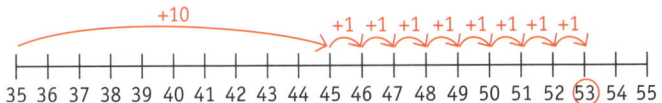

    g   53 + 12 = 65

4. a   40 + 30 = 70
        8 + 9 = 17
        70 + 17 = 87

    b   60 + 20 = 80
        7 + 2 = 9
        80 + 9 = 89

    c   30 + 20 = 50
        7 + 5 = 12
        50 + 12 = 62

    d   10 + 10 = 20
        6 + 6 = 12
        20 + 12 = 32

5. a   50 + 20 = 70
        2 + 4 = 6
        70 + 6 = 76

    b   10 + 30 = 40
        5 + 7 = 12
        40 + 12 = 52

    c   70 + 10 = 80
        2 + 5 = 7
        80 + 7 = 87

    d   20 + 20 = 40
        8 + 8 = 16
        40 + 16 = 56

6. a   7; 7   c   12; 12
    b   10; 10   d   14; 14

7. a   17   c   13   e   19
    b   10   d   12   f   11

8. a   8   b   14   c   19

9. a   31   c   95   e   90
    b   53   d   62   f   33

5. SUBTRACTION

Subtract One-Digit Numbers from Two-Digit Numbers

Page 110 — Your Turn

1. a   25   b   11   c   21   d   33

Page 111 — Practice

1. a   17   e   66   i   72   m   33
    b   30   f   52   j   52   n   39
    c   58   g   22   k   73
    d   22   h   38   l   42

2. a   46   e   17   i   65
    b   36   f   31   j   59
    c   27   g   59
    d   48   h   47

Subtraction with Base-Ten Blocks

Page 113 — Your Turn

1. a   28 – 16 = 12

Page 114 — Practice

1. a   35 – 13 = 22   d   31 – 20 = 11
    b   46 – 14 = 32   e   56 – 24 = 32
    c   22 – 11 = 11

Answers

2. **a** 24 − 11 = 13

b 37 − 26 = 11

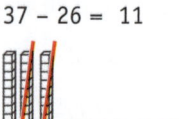

c 47 − 15 = 32

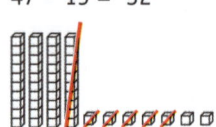

d 32 − 20 = 12

e 43 − 12 = 31

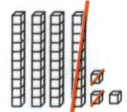

3. **a** 168 − 141 = 27
b 172 − 132 = 40
c 187 − 41 = 146
d 254 − 154 = 100
e 235 − 24 = 211

4. **a** 157 − 41 = 116

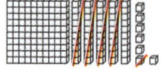

b 138 − 17 = 121

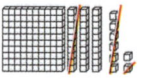

c 184 − 143 = 41

d 127 − 21 = 106

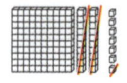

e 244 − 113 = 131

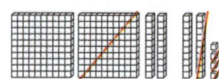

Subtraction with Number Lines

Page 116 — Your Turn

1. **a** 14 − 6 = 8

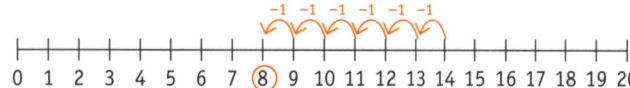

Page 117 — Practice

1. **a** 12 − 4 = 8

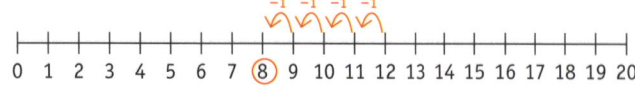

b 11 − 7 = 4

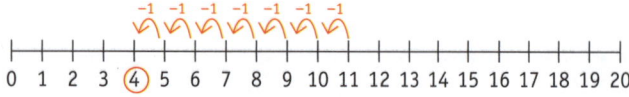

c 18 − 6 = 12

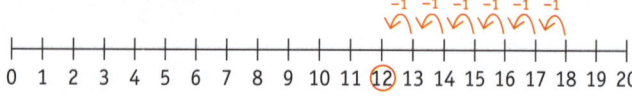

d 14 − 9 = 5

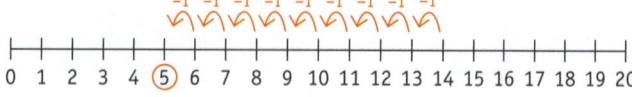

e 17 − 4 = 13

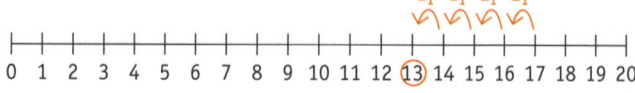

f 20 − 7 = 13

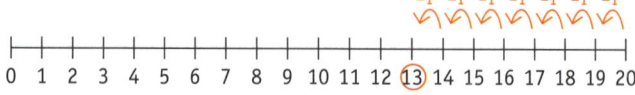

g 18 − 8 = 10

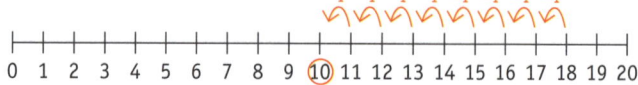

2. **a** 24 − 11 = 13

b 37 − 12 = 25

c 23 − 11 = 12

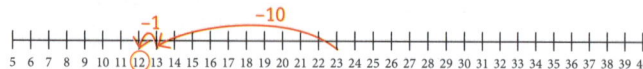

d 35 − 24 = 11

e 44 − 21 = 23

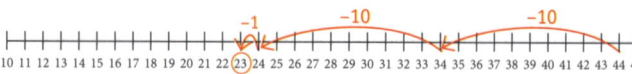

f 39 − 16 = 23

Answers

Subtract Tens and Ones

Page 119 — Your Turn

1. **a** Tens: 70 − 40 = 30
   Ones: 5 − 1 = 4
   Total: 30 + 4 = 34
   75 − 41 = 34

Page 120 — Practice

1. **a** Tens: 40 − 20 = 20
   Ones: 6 − 3 = 3
   Total: 20 + 3 = 23
   46 − 23 = 23

   b Tens: 50 − 30 = 20
   Ones: 4 − 2 = 2
   Total: 20 + 2 = 22
   54 − 32 = 22

   c Tens: 20 − 10 = 10
   Ones: 9 − 5 = 4
   Total: 10 + 4 = 14
   29 − 15 = 14

2. **a** Tens: 90 − 20 = 70
   Ones: 3 − 3 = 0
   Total: 70 + 0 = 70
   93 − 23 = 70

   b Tens: 70 − 30 = 40
   Ones: 4 − 3 = 1
   Total: 40 + 1 = 41
   74 − 33 = 41

   c Tens: 20 − 20 = 0
   Ones: 9 − 0 = 9
   Total: 0 + 9 = 9
   29 − 20 = 9

Add to Subtract

Page 121 — Your Turn

1. **a** 5 + 8 = 13
   13 − 5 = 8

   b 7 + 7 = 14
   14 − 7 = 7

   c 8 + 9 = 17
   17 − 8 = 9

Page 122 — Practice

1. **a** 4   **c** 5   **e** 10
   b 5   **d** 5

2. **a** 5 + 10 = 15
   15 − 5 = 10
   b 4 + 14 = 18
   18 − 4 = 14
   c 9 + 8 = 17
   17 − 9 = 8
   d 11 + 9 = 20
   20 − 11 = 9

e 3 + 8 = 11
11 − 3 = 8

f 5 + 9 = 14
14 − 5 = 9

g 6 + 6 = 12
12 − 6 = 6

Subtraction with Regrouping

Page 123 — Your Turn

1. **a** 25

Page 124 — Practice

1. **a** 48   **c** 37   **e** 19
   b 15   **d** 17

2. **a** 28   **c** 17   **e** 19
   b 17   **d** 15

Standard Subtraction Algorithm

Page 126 — Your Turn

1. **a** 24

Page 127 — Practice

1. **a** 19   **d** 34   **g** 48
   b 19   **e** 19   **h** 68
   c 38   **f** 26   **i** 29

2. **a** 27   **d** 18   **g** 18
   b 41   **e** 29   **h** 24
   c 25   **f** 24   **i** 28

Subtraction with Three-Digit Numbers

Page 129 — Your Turn

1. **a** 435

Page 130 — Practice

1. **a** 216

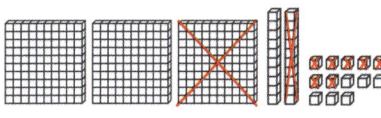

   b 316

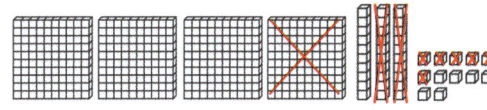

   c 126

Answers

2. a Hundreds: 300 − 200 = 100
       Tens: 50 − 20 = 30
       Ones: 6 − 1 = 5
       Total: 100 + 30 + 5 = 135
   b Hundreds: 600 − 400 = 200
       Tens: 20 − 10 = 10
       Ones: 4 − 2 = 2
       Total: 200 + 10 + 2 = 212
   c Hundreds: 400 − 300 = 100
       Tens: 80 − 50 = 30
       Ones: 2 − 1 = 1
       Total: 100 + 30 + 1 = 131

3. a 167   c 336   e 209
   b 118   d 328

4. a 346   c 109   e 227
   b 209   d 239

Subtraction Review — Page 132

1. a 18   e 27   i 1   m 81
   b 28   f 21   j 43   n 35
   c 49   g 35   k 20
   d 72   h 55   l 29

2. a 48 − 23 = 25   e 149 − 121 = 28
   b 37 − 24 = 13   f 164 − 133 = 31
   c 24 − 14 = 10   g 176 − 32 = 144
   d 39 − 27 = 12   h 232 − 122 = 110

3. a 13 − 5 = 8
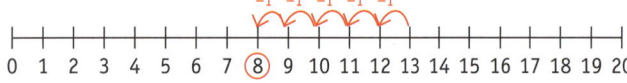
   b 15 − 7 = 8
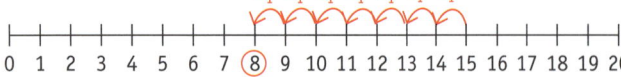
   c 16 − 6 = 10
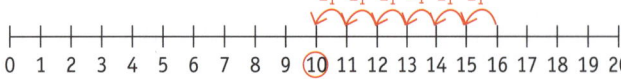
   d 15 − 8 = 7
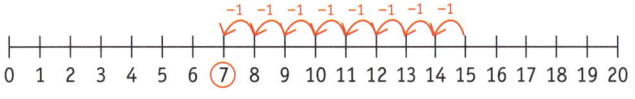

   e 54 − 12 = 42
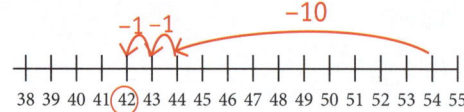
   f 65 − 14 = 51
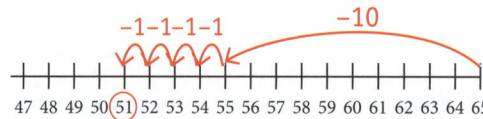
   g 48 − 13 = 35
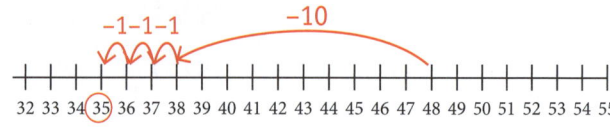

4. a 9 + 9 = 18   d 8 + 7 = 15
      18 − 9 = 9   15 − 8 = 7
   b 7 + 9 = 16   e 6 + 6 = 12
      16 − 7 = 9   12 − 6 = 6
   c 12 + 8 = 20   f 6 + 8 = 14
      20 − 12 = 8   14 − 6 = 8

5. a 6   c 5   e 8
   b 10   d 6   f 7

6. a 29   b 37   c 18   d 26

7. a 37   c 19   e 148
   b 14   d 9   f 17

6. DATA AND GRAPHS

Charts

Page 138 — Your Turn

1. **Goals Scored by Victor's Soccer Team**

Game	Tally	Total
1st Game	|||	3
2nd Game	||||	5
3rd Game	||	2
4th Game		0
5th Game	||	2
6th Game			1

2. a 4th
   b 3rd; 5th
   c 13

238 146444—Catch-Up Math   © Shell Education

Answers

Page 139 — Practice

1.

Room 10's Favorite Types of Books

Type of Book	Tally	Total
fiction	IIII	4
animal facts	IIII I	5
mystery	II	2
adventure	I	1
sports	III	3
comics	IIII I	6
science	IIII	4

2. a adventure   d 5 students
   b fiction; science   e 2 students
   c 25   f 7 students

3.

Room 22's Favorite School Lunches

Type of Lunch	Tally	Total
pizza	IIII III	8
taco	III	3
chicken sandwich	I	1
noodles	III	3
peanut butter and jelly sandwich	III	3
burrito	IIII	4
fish sticks	II	2

4. a chicken sandwich   d 6 students
   b taco, noodles, peanut butter and jelly sandwich   e 1 student
   f 4 students
   c 24

Picture Graphs

Page 141 — Your Turn

1. a hockey

Page 142 — Practice

1. **Flowers in the School Garden**

tulip	🌷🌷🌷
rose	🌷🌷🌷🌷🌷🌷
lily	🌷
iris	🌷🌷🌷

Key: 🌷 = 1 flower

2. a iris   d 14 flowers
   b 5 roses   e rose
   c 7 tulips and irises

3. **Students' Favorite Pets**

dog	♥♥♥
cat	♥♥♥♥
hamster	♥
rabbit	♥½

Key: ♥ = 2 students

4. a hamster   c hamster
   b 6 students   d 3 students

5. **Students' Favorite Recess Activities**

swings	★★★★★
baseball	★★★
monkey bars	★★
tag	★★

Key: ★ = 1 student

6. a tag   c tag
   b 1 student   d 13 students

Bar Graphs

Page 146 — Your Turn

1. a winter   d 1 student
   b 13 students   e 15 students
   c 5 students   f 28 students

Page 147 — Practice

1. a writing   d 4 students
   b 7 students   e 12 students
   c 1 student   f 19 students

© Shell Education   146444—Catch-Up Math   239

Answers

2.

Room 18's Favorite Subjects

Subject	Tally Marks	Total
reading	|||||	5
math	||||| ||	7
writing	|||	3
science	||||	4

3.
- **a** candy
- **b** 7 students
- **c** 6 students
- **d** 13 students
- **e** 19 students

4.
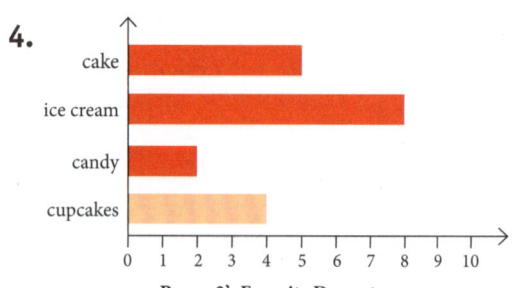

5.
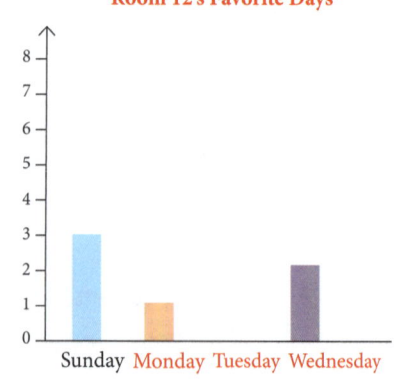

6. Check that questions can be answered by the data. Check that answers are correct.

Line Plots

Page 151 — Your Turn

1.
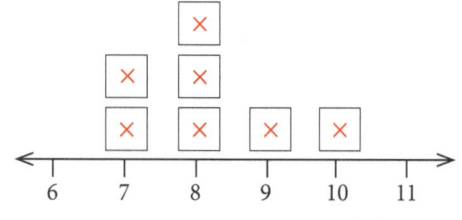

2.
- **a** 0 days
- **b** 2 days
- **c** 2 days

Page 152 — Practice

1.
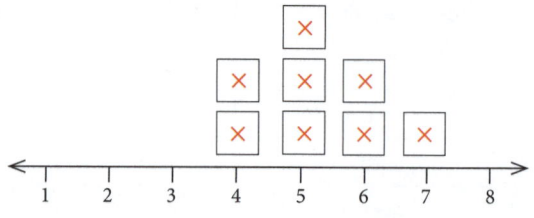

2.
- **a** There are no muffins that have only 1, 2, or 3 blueberries.
- **b** 3 muffins
- **c** 7 blueberries
- **d** 4 blueberries
- **e** 8 muffins

3.
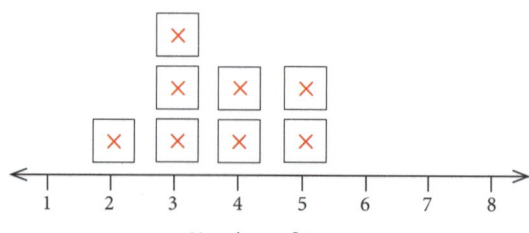

4.
- **a** 2 players
- **b** 3 players
- **c** 2 laps
- **d** 5 laps
- **e** 4 players

5.
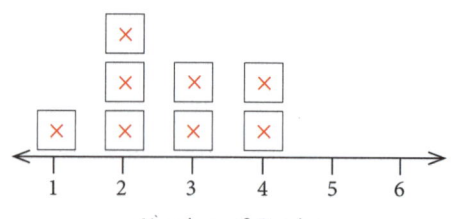

6. Check that questions can be answered by the data. Check that answers are correct.

Data and Graphs Review — Page 155

1.
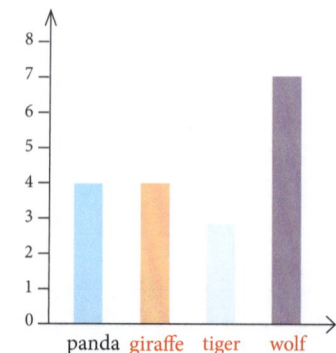

Answers

2. **a** wolf
   b tiger
   c 4 students
   d 7 students

3. Check that questions can be answered by the data. Check that answers are correct.

4. **Room 1's Choice Time Activities**

Key: 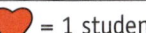 = 1 student

5. Check that questions can be answered by the data. Check that answers are correct.

6. **Children at the After-School Club**

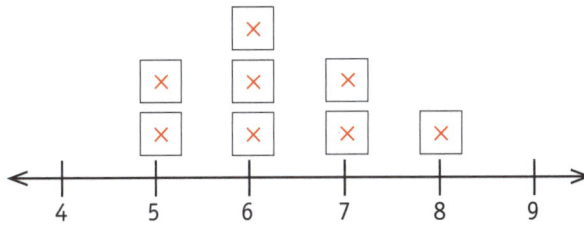

7. **a** 2 children
   b 3 children
   c 8 years old
   d None of the children are 4 or 9 years old.
   e 5 years old

8. **Syllables in Names**

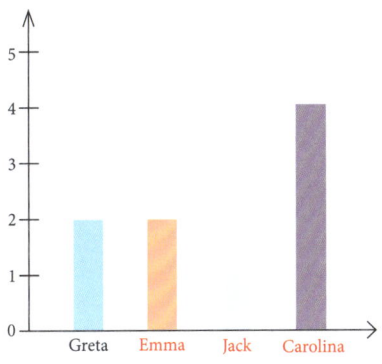

7. SHAPES AND ARRAYS

Shape Attributes

Page 159 — Your Turn

1.

Page 160 — Practice

1. **a** Students should draw a quadrilateral.
   b Students should draw a hexagon.
   c Students should draw a pentagon.
   d Students should draw a quadrilateral with equal sides.
   e Students should draw a quadrilateral.

2. Check that shapes have the listed attributes.

Make New Shapes

Page 161 — Your Turn

1. **a**

Page 162 — Practice

1. **a** two squares
   b a rectangle and two squares
   c two trapezoids
   d three triangles

2. Check that each set of shapes is used in a composite shape.

3. Check that a house has been drawn using shapes.

Answers

Understanding Arrays

Page 164 — Your Turn

1. **a**   2 rows

   5 columns

   10 total circles

Page 165 — Practice

1. **a** Total: 16

   b Total: 10

   c Total: 15

   d Total: 12

   e Total: 8

   f Total: 12

   g Total: 12

Arrays with Rectangles

Page 166 — Your Turn

1. **a**

Page 167 — Practice

1. **a** 12 parts   **c** 16 parts   **e** 8 parts

   b 10 parts   **d** 15 parts

Add Arrays

Page 168 — Your Turn

1. **a**   2 + 2 + 2 = 6   **b**   4 + 4 = 8

Page 169 — Practice

1. **a** Rows: 3 + 3 + 3 = 9

   Columns: 3 + 3 + 3 = 9

   b Rows: 2 + 2 + 2 + 2 + 2 = 10

   Columns: 5 + 5 = 10

   c Rows: 6 + 6 = 12

   Columns: 2 + 2 + 2 + 2 + 2 + 2 = 12

   d Rows: 3 + 3 + 3 + 3 + 3 = 15

   Columns: 5 + 5 + 5 = 15

   e Rows: 3 + 3 + 3 + 3 = 12

   Columns: 4 + 4 + 4 = 12

Shapes and Arrays Review — Page 170

1. Check that 6 composite shapes have been created.

2. **a**

   total: 10

   b

   total: 9

3. **a**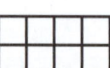

   b

   c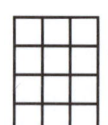

   d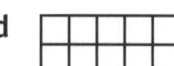

4. **a** Rows: 6 + 6 + 6 = 18

   Columns: 3 + 3 + 3 + 3 + 3 + 3 = 18

   b Rows: 2 + 2 = 4

   Columns: 2 + 2 = 4

   c Rows: 4 + 4 + 4 + 4 + 4 = 20

   Columns: 5 + 5 + 5 + 5 = 20

   d Rows: 2 + 2 + 2 = 6

   Columns: 3 + 3 = 6

Answers

8. FRACTIONS

Equal Parts

Page 172 — Your Turn

1. **a** halves **b** fourths **c** thirds

Page 173 — Practice

1. a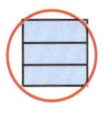

   b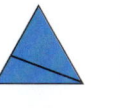

   c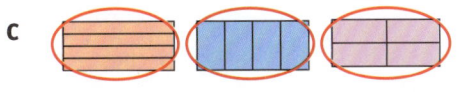

2. Check that shapes are correctly divided into even sections.

Partition Rectangles

Page 174 — Your Turn

Check that the rectangles have been divided evenly.

Page 175 — Practice

Check that rectangles are divided in different ways and correctly show the given fractions.

1. a

   b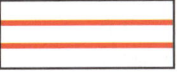

2.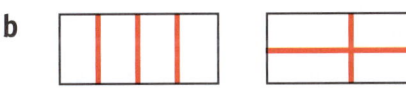
 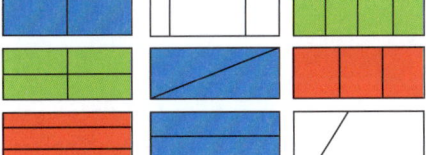

Partition Circles

Page 176 — Your Turn

1. **a** fourths **b** thirds

Page 177 — Practice

1. Check that rectangles are divided in different ways and correctly show the given fractions.

2.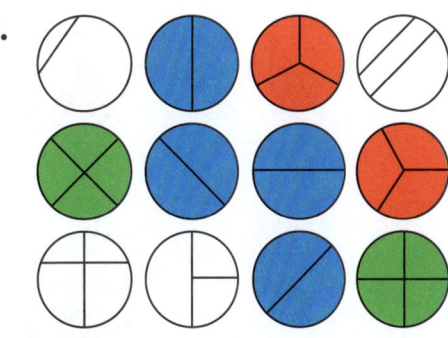

Naming Fractions

Page 178 — Your Turn

1. **a** two-thirds

Page 179 — Practice

Check that the correct number of parts are shaded. They can be shaded in any configuration.

1. a 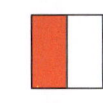 f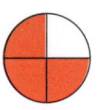

   b 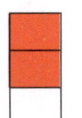 g

   c 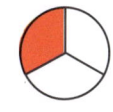 h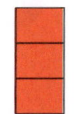

   d i

   e

2. Possible answer: The number of parts shaded is the same as the number of equal parts in the whole.

Answers

3. a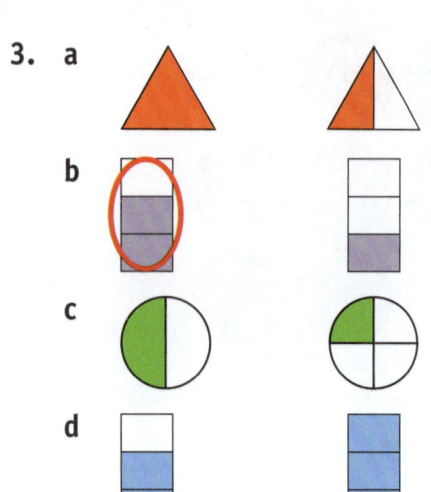
   b
   c
   d
   e

4. a four-fourths   b two-halves

Fractions Review — Page 181
1.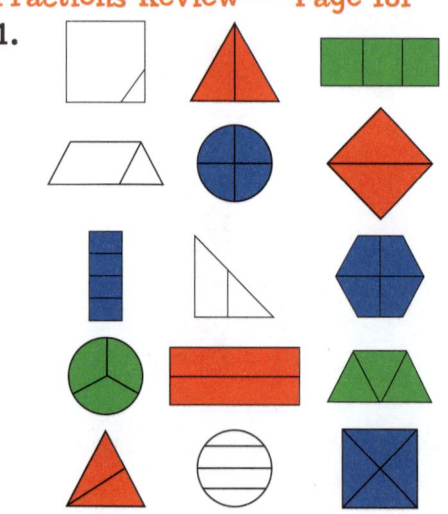

2. Check that shapes are correctly divided into the given fractions.

3. Check that the correct number of parts are shaded. They can be shaded in any configuration.

   a 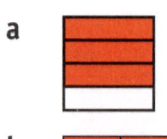   c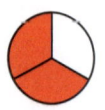
   b   d

4. Check that shapes are drawn, divided, and shaded correctly.

9. LENGTH

Measurement Tools
Page 184 — Your Turn
1. a ruler   b measuring tape

Page 185 — Practice
1. Check that reasonable tools are circled. Possible answers:
   a ruler   e ruler
   b yardstick   f ruler
   c measuring tape   g measuring tape
   d yardstick

2. a yards   f inches
   b inches   g centimeters
   c feet   h yards
   d centimeters   i meters
   e centimeters

Measurement Units
Page 187 — Your Turn
1. a 15 base-ten blocks
       8 cubes

Page 188 — Practice
1. a 7 base-ten blocks   c 18 base-ten blocks
       4 cubes   10 cubes
   b 4 base-ten blocks   d 4 base-ten blocks
       2 cubes   2 cubes

2. a 2 inches   c 7 inches
       5 centimeters   18 centimeters
   b 10 inches   d 4 inches
       25 centimeters   10 centimeters

Inches and Centimeters
Page 190 — Your Turn
1. a 8 inches

Page 191 — Practice
1. a 3 inches   b 6 inches   c 2 inches
2. a 1 centimeter
   b 5 centimeters
   c 8 centimeters

244   146444—Catch-Up Math   © Shell Education

Answers

Compare Lengths

Page 192 — Your Turn

1. a The carrot is longer than the banana.
   b The flower is shorter than the branch.

Page 193 — Practice

1. a    d

   b    e

   c

2. a  d

   b  e

   c

3. a 2 inches longer   d 6 inches longer
   b 3 inches longer   e 2 inches longer
   c 2 inches longer

Estimate Lengths

Page 195 — Your Turn

1. a 4 inches   c 2 yards or meters
   b 100 yards or meters

Page 196 — Practice

1. a 18 centimeters
   b 10 inches
   c 15 inches
   d 1 yard
   e 7 inches

2. a 2 a notebook
      3 a nail
      1 a doorway
   b 2 a desk
      1 a playground slide
      3 a sheet of notebook paper
   c 2 a soccer ball
      1 a fence
      3 a crayon

Length Word Problems

Page 197 — Your Turn

1. a 14 – 7 = 7 inches

Page 198 — Practice

1. a 25 + 22 = 47 inches
   b 16 – 9 = 7 centimeters
   c 18 + 15 = 33 feet
   d 22 + 14 = 36 yards
   e 53 – 37 = 16 feet
   f 27 – 14 = 13 feet

Length Review — Page 199

1. Check that students circled a reasonable tool. Possible answers:
   a measuring tape   c ruler
   b ruler   d yardstick

2. a inches   c feet
   b centimeters   d meters

3. Check that reasonable objects are drawn for the given lengths.

4. a

   b

   c

   d

© Shell Education   146444—Catch-Up Math   245

Answers

5. a
    b
    c
    d

6. Check that answers are reasonable.

7. a 4 inches longer   b 3 inches longer

8. a 6 inches   d 50 yards
    b 8 inches   e 40 feet
    c 14 centimeters   f 1 inch

9. a 5 inches   d 12 centimeters
    b 10 inches   e 3 inches
    c 6 centimeters   f 7 inches

10. a 20 centimeters
       8 inches
    b 15 centimeters
       6 inches

11. a 10 base-ten blocks
       6 cubes
    b 18 base-ten blocks
       10 cubes

12. a 12 + 13 = 25 feet
    b 15 − 9 = 6 feet
    c 30 − 21 = 9 centimeters
    d 12 + 6 = 18 inches
    e 12 − 10 = 2 inches
    f 50 − 43 = 7 feet
    g 26 + 32 = 58 feet

10. TIME AND MONEY

Digital Clocks

Page 205 — Your Turn

1. a seven thirty-five   c three forty
    b eleven twenty

Page 206 — Practice

1. a six fifteen   d three ten
    b eleven forty   e seven twenty
    c five fifty-five

2. a 8:20   d 12:15
    b 3:00   e 9:40
    c 4:30

3. a two forty   d ten fifteen
    b twelve forty   e one ten
    c six o'clock

Analog Clocks: 00 and 30

Page 207 — Your Turn

1. a 1:00

Page 208 — Practice

1. a 1:30   c 6:30   e 8:30
    b 6:00   d 4:00

2. a    d
    b    e
    c

Analog Clocks: 15 and 45

Page 209 — Your Turn

1. a 12:15   b 4:15   c 6:45

Page 210 — Practice

1. a 8:15   c 12:45   e 6:15
    b 2:15   d 4:45

2. a  c  e

b  d

Five-Minute Intervals

Page 211 — Your Turn

1. a 5:10

Page 212 — Practice

1. a 9:40   c 1:50   e 2:25

b 2:55   d 6:45

2. a 10:35   c 3:50

b 5:35   d 6:20

Elapsed Time

Page 213 — Your Turn

1. a   30 minutes

Page 214 — Practice

1. a

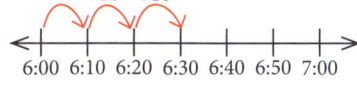

1:30

b

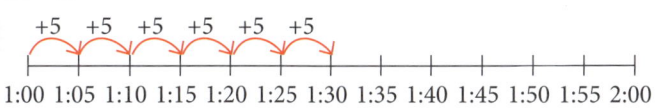

6:00

c

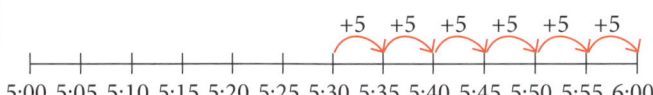

1 hour or 60 minutes

d

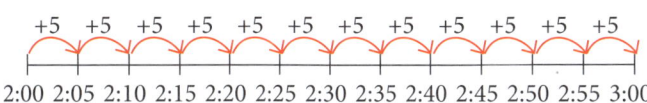

5:30

e

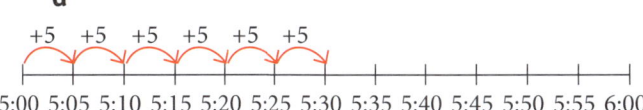

30 minutes

Adding Coins

Page 215 — Your Turn

1. a 33¢   b 30¢

Page 216 — Practice

1. a 36¢   d 18¢   g $1.32

b 45¢   e 50¢   h $1.38

c 22¢   f $1.40   i $2.30

Money Word Problems

Page 217 — Your Turn

1. a 50¢ – 15¢ = 35¢   b 10¢ + 20¢ = 30¢

Page 218 — Practice

1. a 52¢ + 42¢ = 94¢

b 80¢ – 30¢ = 50¢

c $3.00 – $1.00 = $2.00

d 20¢ + 10¢ + 3¢ = 33¢

Yes, Eli has enough money because 33¢ is more than 25¢.

e Hank: 75¢ + 2¢ = 77¢

Paula: 50¢ + 30¢ = 80¢

Paula has more money.

f 100¢ + 50¢ + 30¢ + 5¢ = 185¢ or $1.85

Time and Money Review — Page 219

1. a 2:30   c 3:15   e 7:35

b 4:00   d 6:45   f 9:50

2. a  c  e

b  d  f

3. a 10:10   c 6:00   e 3:00

b 12:40   d 2:15   f 11:30

Answers

4.   a   4:30   c   8:15   e   9:10
      b   10:20   d   7:00   f   12:00

5.   a   34¢   e   45¢   i $1.40
      b   25¢   f   70¢   j $1.42
      c   34¢   g   49¢
      d   35¢   h $1.17

6.   a

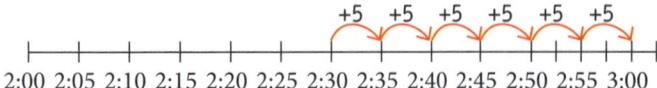

3:00

      b

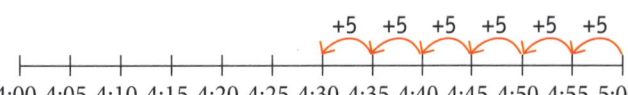

4:30

7.   a   27¢ + 51¢ = 78¢
      b   75¢ − 25¢ = 50¢
      c $20.00 − $4.00 = $16.00
      d   40¢ + 10¢ + 4¢ = 54¢